AME Year 11 English Workbook

NCEA Level 1

A write-in workbook with brief revision notes covering all Achievement Standards for the NCEA Level 1 English course.

NCEA-format questions, with full answers detailing NCEA grades (Achieved, Merit, Excellence) are provided for all externally assessed Achievement Standards.

Jeanette Duffy

Cindy Ford

ESA Publications (NZ) Ltd

AME Year 11 English Workbook

NCEA Level 1

Jeanette Duffy and Cindy Ford

ESA Publications (NZ) Ltd

ISBN 1-877291-72-2

First published in 2000 by ESA Publications (NZ) Ltd
This fourth, NCEA Level 1 edition published in New Zealand in 2003 by ESA Publications (NZ) Ltd

Copyright © Jeanette Duffy and Cindy Ford, 2003
Copyright © ESA Publications (NZ) Ltd, 2003

This book is copyright.

Many of the questions used in this book are adapted or taken directly from recent NZQA examinations. All these questions are reproduced with the permission of NZQA, who own copyright in the questions.

The selection and arrangement of the questions and the solutions and tips are entirely the responsibility of the authors.

The questions in this book include the 2002 Externals and others in NCEA format and the answers to these questions have A, M and E grades. The assignment of grades is entirely the responsibility of the authors and has been made according to the best judgement of the authors at the time of writing.

No part of this publication may be stored or transmitted in any form or by any means, electronic or mechanical, including recording or storage of any information in a retrieval system, without permission in writing from the publisher.

No reproduction may be made, whether by photocopying or any other means, unless a written licence has been obtained from the publisher or its agent, Copyright Licensing Ltd, freephone 0800-480 271 or www.copyright.co.nz.

Infringements will be prosecuted.

Information relating to the Achievement Standards and Exemplars is taken from the NZQA website and is current at the time of publication. ESA Publications (NZ) Ltd does not take any responsibility for any subsequent changes to the Achievement Standards, Exemplars or exam format. Should a student have any concerns, they should:
- Check with their teacher.
- Check the NZQA website by selecting 'For education professionals' at www.nzqa.govt.nz/ncea/

ESA Publications (NZ) Ltd
Box 9453, Newmarket, Auckland, New Zealand
Phone: 09 579 3126
Fax: 09 579 4713
Freephone: 0800 372 266
Freefax: 0800 329 372
Email: info@esa.co.nz
Internet: www.esa.co.nz

Editor: Terry Bunn
Compositor: Barnaby McBryde
Proofreader: Dina Cloete

Printed in New Zealand

Contents

Introduction i
    Using this Workbook ii
    Study Techniques/Revising iv
    Learning During the Year v
    Preparation for Externally Assessed NCEA Level 1 Assessments..................... v

Achievement Standard 1.1
    Produce creative writing... 1

Achievement Standard 1.2
    Produce formal writing... 9

Achievement Standard 1.3
    Read, study and understand an extended written text.................................. 21

Achievement Standard 1.4
    Read, study and understand a number of short written texts....................... 37

Achievement Standard 1.5
    Read, study and understand a visual or oral text.. 49

Achievement Standard 1.6
    Read and show understanding of unfamiliar texts 67

Achievement Standard 1.7
    Deliver a speech in a formal situation 77

Achievement Standard 1.8
    Produce a media or dramatic presentation 83

Achievement Standard 1.9
    Research, organise and present information 93

Answers
    1.1 103
    1.2 104
    1.3 105
    1.4 108
    1.5 111
    1.6 115
    1.7 116
    1.8 116
    1.9 117

Keyword List.. 121

© ESA Publications (NZ) Ltd, Freephone 0800-372 266

Introduction

Each Achievement Standard is worth a certain number of credits. If you achieve the Standard (that is, your grade is either 'Achieved', 'Merit' or 'Excellence') you have earned that number of credits toward your NCEA qualification. You need a minimum of 80 Level 1 Credits in order to achieve a Level 1 NCEA Certificate.

In English, the following Achievement Standards are available at NCEA Level 1.

Title	Description	Credits	Internal/External
English 1.1	Produce creative writing	3	Internal
English 1.2	Produce formal writing	3	External
English 1.3	Read, study and understand an extended written text	2	External
English 1.4	Read, study and understand a number of short written texts	2	External
English 1.5	Read, study and understand a visual or oral text	2	External
English 1.6	Read and show understanding of unfamiliar texts	3	External
English 1.7	Deliver a speech in a formal situation	3	Internal
English 1.8	Produce a media or dramatic presentation	3	Internal
English 1.9	Research, organise and present information	3	Internal

A **keyword list** is included in the back of the book. Use this list of key words to check the meanings of important terms.

Internally Assessed Achievement Standards for NCEA Level 1 English

There are four internally assessed Achievement Standards:

- Achievement Standard 1.1 'Produce creative writing.'

  Assessment for this Achievement Standard will require developing idea(s) convincingly with detail in a piece of creative writing, using a controlled writing style and structuring material clearly and effectively in a way that is appropriate to audience, purpose and text type, and using writing conventions accurately.

- Achievement Standard 1.7 'Deliver a speech in a formal situation.'

  Assessment for this Achievement Standard will require speaking in a formal situation to communicate convincing ideas with supporting detail and explanation, structuring content and using language and a level of formality appropriate to audience and purpose, with effect, and speaking audibly to an audience with confidence and impact consistently using voice, eye contact and body language for deliberate effect.

- Achievement Standard 1.8 'Produce a media or dramatic presentation.'

  Assessment for this Achievement Standard will require communicating fully developed ideas in a presentation for a specific audience and purpose, using appropriate verbal and visual/dramatic techniques with striking and/or original effect, and identifying verbal and visual/dramatic techniques used and their intended effect.

- Achievement Standard 1.9 'Research, organise and present information.'

  Assessment for this Achievement Standard will require planning research by stating the topic, posing key questions and identifying possible sources, collecting, selecting and recording relevant information, and recording sources in an accepted format and recording the steps taken during the research process.

Start working on internal Achievement Standards as soon as you receive the task from your teacher. Develop a timeline for completion by the due date.

Make sure you build in time to review your work and make changes if necessary. This could include rehearsal time for speeches/dramatic performances.

Externally Assessed Achievement Standards for NCEA Level 1 English

All five externally assessed Achievement Standards will be pen-and-paper exam assessments and total 12 credits.

It is vital that all questions should be attempted.

A suggested time allocation if you are sitting all five externally assessed Achievement Standards is: AS 1.2 45 minutes; AS 1.3 25 minutes; AS 1.4 25 minutes; AS 1.5 25 minutes; AS 1.6 60 minutes.

Free Study Planner

Planning your end-of-year revision is vital. You must allow enough time to revise and prepare for all subjects. The ESA Term 4 study planner is a popular A3-sized, two-colour planner which can be used anytime from the start of the Term 3 school holidays. It is highly recommended.

The planner is free (while stocks last):

- With any ESA title purchased direct from ESA in Term 3 or Term 4.
- With any bulk quantities purchased by teachers or schools for students.
- By sending a stamped, self-addressed envelope to ESA Box 9453, Newmarket, Auckland.

Using this Workbook

Workbook features

- This workbook can be used at any time of the year. During the school year, you could use it as your teacher covers each Achievement Standard. Alternatively, use it toward the end of the year in Term 4 as part of your external Achievement Standards preparation and revision.
- The Assessment Specifications for each Achievement Standard are shown in the beginning of each chapter. These describe the types of requirements or questions you can expect to find in each Achievement Standard.
- The criteria for awarding 'Achieved', 'Merit' and 'Excellence' are given in the beginning of each chapter.
- Most of the questions have lines and spaces for you to write in your answers – however, you may need to continue on your own paper.

Step 1: Getting to know this Workbook

This workbook has been written for students studying **English** at **NCEA Level 1**. It is intended as a useful self-study guide which should be used alongside class textbooks, the ESA Study Guide, class notes and other assignment tasks, etc.

Each Achievement Standard is covered in one chapter.

Externally assessed Achievement Standards

Each chapter contains:

- Brief revision notes. These cover what you should know and include worked examples.
- Tasks to help you prepare your knowledge base for the exam. These Tasks often take you through, step-by-step, how to answer NCEA Level 1 English questions. Answer spaces are provided.
- Questions of an NCEA Level 1 English standard and format. Each answer for these questions has an NCEA grading – 'Achieved', 'Merit' and/or 'Excellence'. Explanations for answers are sometimes given.

Internally assessed Achievement Standards

Each chapter contains brief notes that will explain the Achievement Standard and provide tips on how to gain the best NCEA grading.

There are Tasks to complete to help understanding and preparation for your internal assessment requirements.

Step 2: Answering NCEA questions for external Achievement Standards

- Work through the questions, making some attempt to answer even if you are not sure – as you might in an exam. Where necessary go to the keyword lists or the ESA Study Guide for further information.
- Follow the instructions. Answer the question fully.
- Have the attitude that you have the necessary skills.
- The questions in the workbook are designed to make you think. It is okay to make mistakes, as long as you learn from your mistakes. That is part of the learning process.
- Make sure you answer every part of every question. You will not lose anything for a wrong answer, but you certainly cannot gain any credit if you leave a blank. If necessary, take a sensible guess based on what you understand from the rest of the question.
- Answer spaces are not provided for the NCEA questions requiring an essay-style answer, but the model answers in the Tasks provide a guide as to appropriate lengths for answers. The answer spaces for the short-answer NCEA questions should provide a guide as to how much working or writing is expected.

Step 3: Marking questions

> The letters *A*, *M*, *E*, in the answers section stand for the grades 'Achieved', 'Merit, and 'Excellence', and offer the highest level of evidence the answer to the question is expected to provide.

- Take the time to compare your work carefully with the answers at the back of the book.
- Model answers for each Practice Question for literature will probably not be on *your* text; however, look closely at the structure and level of supporting detail provided.
- Allocate grades to the answers yourself or go to your teacher. Keep a record of your grades and set your own expectations of how you want to do in the Achievement Standards.

Step 4: Timing questions

- Working through the questions in this workbook will help you get used to the requirements of the external assessments so that you can work with increasing speed and accuracy.
- Learn how much time you can spend per question. Work to that time in your revision sessions.
- Timing how long it takes to answer each question is critical. If you run over time on one question it means that you will have to rush through another question. A rushed question could well result in you getting a lower grade than you are capable of.

Study Techniques/Revising

Step 1: Creating the learning environment
You need your own study space, with a suitable desk and chair which allow an upright sitting posture – this will keep you alert and comfortable and aid concentration. Good lighting and adequate ventilation are essential. Ensure your study area is free from distractions, such as the radio/stereo and television, and interruptions such as the phone and other family members. Take a 10-minute break after every 50 minutes of study – be disciplined about this as a longer break will make it difficult to continue where you left off.

Step 2: Organise your study area
Arrange all the material you require in an orderly manner. Use folders and file boxes to organise and store your notes, handouts and assignments. Leave your desk tidy each time you complete a study session; that way it will be a simple matter of sitting down to commence your next study session.

Step 3: Set up a regular study pattern
Study is an on-going activity throughout the year. You should not leave it until just before exams (external assessments) to study your work.

Step 4: Check what you already know
- Decide on a topic you want to study from the subject you are revising. It may be useful to start where you feel knowledgeable. This will give you confidence and will be a good lead-in to more challenging sections.
- Before doing any study activities, check over your notes and refresh your memory. This will reactivate what you already know.

Step 5: Revision for NCEA Level 1 English
There are five externally assessed Achievement Standards:
- Read through your notes on each Achievement Standard and create study notes on the important information needed for your answers (for example, quotations, features of a specific character, notes on a specific theme). Putting these notes into an exercise book will ensure easy access.
- Memorise important information – you could repeatedly write out the notes, recite the notes out loud, or get family members to test you.
- Write a number of practice answers, ensuring you include all relevant information necessary to fully answer the questions. (You could ask your classroom teacher to mark these for you.)
- Practise your time management skills. Write answers in the time allocated for each question in the exam. With practice, your speed will improve.

Learning During the Year

1. Ensure you understand the year's work as it is covered in class. Ask your teacher if you are unsure, or use the ESA Study Guide to check work and as an at-home backup to classroom work.

2. Carefully choose who you sit by in class. Avoid inattentive or distracting friends, fun though they may be. Sit by people who participate in classroom activities, who work hard and who intend doing well at school.

3. Complete your assignments on time.

4. Get into a good homework routine. You should be doing 1–2 hours per night during Terms 1 and 2 and at least 2 hours per night during Term 3. By Term 4 you should be doing 2–3 hours per night, including revision for exams.

5. Maintain your participation in sporting, cultural, leisure and family activities to balance your school studies.

Preparation for the Externally Assessed NCEA Level 1 Assessments

Revision for external assessments/exams is like any other training – it involves careful planning and thorough preparation. Covering all the chapters on the externally assessed Achievement Standards in this book should ensure you will be confident to give your best performance.

Stay healthy – practise healthy habits during the period of the exam preparation – eat well, take regular exercise and have at least eight hours' sleep each night.

- *Prepare your equipment for the exam.*
  Pens, blue or black *(not red or green)*.
  Ruler.
  Exam slip *(if required)*.
- Check you know where to go to and what time to be there. *This should be on your Term 4 timetable.*
- The night before the exam ensure you have a good night's sleep. Have a good breakfast on the morning of the exam.
- Familiarise yourself with the exam format. There are five separate papers – one for each externally assessed NCEA Level 1 English Achievement Standard.

In the Exam

Nervousness: Nervousness is to be expected and is quite normal. If you need to, use an easy, effective relaxation technique, such as deep breathing.

Hard questions: Do not be put off by a hard question – others will be finding the same thing.

Order of answering: You can answer the Achievement Standards in any order. Begin with something you feel most confident with.

Allocate sufficient time: You should now know how long to spend on a question. Stick with this. Avoid going 'over time' on a question. When you have used up your allocated time, move on to the next question.

Attempt every question: Apply the lessons you learnt in completing this book.

Answers are to be written on the question paper in the spaces provided. Read the questions carefully and follow the instructions. Take the time to 'brainstorm' where appropriate.

Write quality answers: Use the following information to help you to write appropriate answers to questions in the exam.

- Read questions carefully so you understand what is being asked for. Follow the instructions carefully.
- Neatness – write tidily, using blue or black pen. If the exam marker is unable to read an untidy script, they are not allowed to 'mind read' – they must mark only what they see on your paper. Errors or 'changes of mind' should be crossed out (do not use 'Twink').

Check Answers: If you have time, check your answers. Avoid leaving an exam early. Remember to go back to partly completed and unanswered questions and try to complete them.

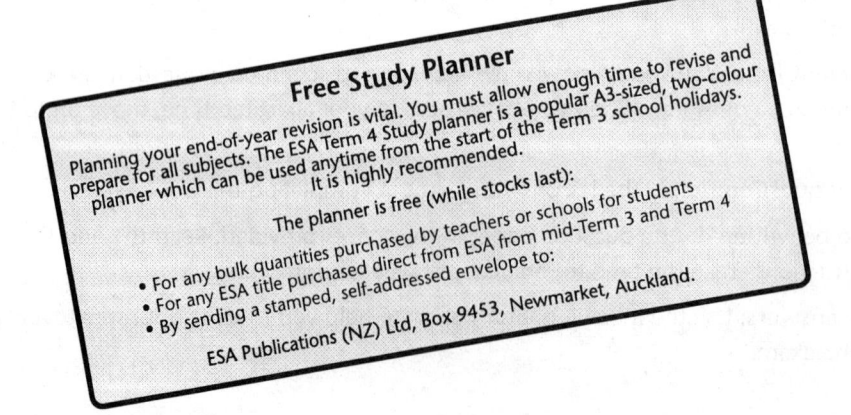

Free Study Planner

Planning your end-of-year revision is vital. You must allow enough time to revise and prepare for all subjects. The ESA Term 4 Study planner is a popular A3-sized, two-colour planner which can be used anytime from the start of the Term 3 school holidays. It is highly recommended.

The planner is free (while stocks last):

- For any bulk quantities purchased by teachers or schools for students
- For any ESA title purchased direct from ESA from mid-Term 3 and Term 4
- By sending a stamped, self-addressed envelope to:

ESA Publications (NZ) Ltd, Box 9453, Newmarket, Auckland.

Produce creative writing

NCEA Achievement Standard 1.1
Internally assessed
3 credits

Achievement Standard 1.1 focuses on four main skill areas – your ability to:
- Develop ideas.
- Write in an original, creative manner.
- Structure material effectively.
- Proofread your work for accuracy in spelling, punctuation and grammar.

Your teacher will select a specific topic for you to write on and will provide you with clear instructions. You will be required to write in excess of 300 words.

The assessed **skills** that follow remain the same across all schools and all topics.

Assessment criteria

Achieved	Merit	Excellence
Express **idea(s)** with **detail** in a piece of creative writing.	*Develop* **idea(s)** with **detail** in a piece of creative writing.	Develop **idea(s)** *convincingly* with *detail* in a piece of creative writing.
Use a writing **style** appropriate to audience, purpose and text type.	Use a *controlled* writing **style** appropriate to audience, purpose and text type.	Use a controlled writing **style** appropriate to audience, purpose and text type, and *which commands attention*.
Structure material in a way that is appropriate to audience, purpose and text type.	**Structure** material *clearly* in a way that is appropriate to audience, purpose and text type.	**Structure** material clearly and *effectively* in a way that is appropriate to audience, purpose and text type.
Use **writing conventions** without intrusive errors.	Use **writing conventions** *accurately*.	Use **writing conventions** *accurately*.

Skill 1 – Ideas

Ideas include thoughts/feelings, experiences, responses.

- **(A):** Express idea(s) with **detail** in a piece of creative writing.
- **(M):** **Develop** idea(s) with detail in a piece of creative writing.
- **(E):** Develop idea(s) **convincingly** with detail in a piece of creative writing.

To build on a single idea by adding detail; link that idea to other ideas and details

The inclusion of description, information, etc

Believable and credible

Ideas are the heart of your piece of writing – if you want to do well you must take the time to thoroughly brainstorm your ideas and really think about how you will develop them before you start writing the actual description.

2 English Achievement Standard 1.1

Step 1: *Brainstorm your chosen focus* before you start writing your description

It may help to divide your brainstorm into **concrete details** (absolutes, ie unquestionable facts) and **feelings** associated with the person, place, or focus of the piece of writing.

> The Example topic '**Describe a special person in your life**' will be used throughout this chapter. The Example focuses on someone's grandmother.

Concrete details	Feelings
Warm and loving	Love her deeply
Has difficulty walking/moving	Proud of Nana
Is now very old	Feel for her being 'trapped by her body'
Snores loudly	Amazed at her determination/spirit
Gasps for breath sometimes	Sad for her
Uses a walking stick	etc
Was beautiful in her youth	
Always independent	
etc	

Task 1

Practise developing ideas with either:
- a special person of your own choice, or
- the actual topic given to you by your teacher.

Brainstorm your chosen focus (ie general initial ideas).

Concrete details	Feelings

Step 2: *Decide what the purpose of your piece of writing is;* what you are specifically trying to communicate

- What's important about your grandmother?
- What matters to you about her / what is special about her?
- What to you want to communicate about her?

These form your **ideas** – what it is you are trying to say

The Example piece of writing will focus on communicating the ideas that:
- Nana is a warm, special person.
- Nana was beautiful and spirited in her youth.
- Nana is now very old and physically fragile.
- Nana's spirit has not changed.

Task 2

Decide what specifically you are trying to communicate; what the purpose of your piece of writing is.

- _____
- _____
- _____
- _____

Step 3: Brainstorm how you will develop the key ideas

Development involves how you will build on the idea; what detail you will add, what other ideas you could link the idea to.

Idea	Development and details
Nana is a warm special person	• Talk about her eyes, how they are warm • Could link to a photograph of her in her youth (and describe her) • Mention the radiance that shines out from her wedding photo
Nana was beautiful and spirited in her youth	• Describe wedding photo • Describe hair • Skin • Personality is stamped on her face
Nana is now old and fragile	• The way she walks; her walking stick • Her coughing and snoring • The way she gasps for breath • Her wrinkles

Use your very first brainstorm to help with this.

Task 3

Use the topic you chose in **Task 1** to brainstorm how you will **develop** your key ideas.

Idea	Development and details

Skill 2 – Style

The writing must suit the requirements of the task

- **(A):** Use a writing style **appropriate** to audience, purpose and text type.
- **(M):** Use a **controlled** writing style appropriate to audience, purpose and text type.
- **(E):** Use a controlled writing style appropriate to audience, purpose and text type, and which **commands attention**.

Has thought carefully about expression, use of language, description, etc

Original, effective incorporation of figurative language, sentence variety, vocabulary choice – shows a flair for language

The style of your writing is something you should work on, draft, reshape and continue to change until your writing shows control and crafting. The **style list** may include:

- Specific poetic devices – such as personification, simile, metaphor.
- Specific sound device – such as alliteration and onomatopoeia.
- Specific language – devices such as deliberate repetition.
- A variety of sentence types and lengths.
- Carefully chosen verbs.
- Carefully chosen adjectives and adverbs.

Concentrate on 'showing' not 'telling' – rather than telling the reader something directly, try and incorporate action or speech to portray the idea. For example, instead of telling the reader 'The man was greedy and money hungry', you could show this by using detail 'He snatched back the gold card and squirrelled it away in his wallet'.

Creating a good piece of writing is like creating an original piece of music, or shaping a unique piece of art; it takes time and thought and a lot of reworking!

Task 4

This is based upon the Example topic (Grandmother).

Read the extracts taken from the piece of writing 'The Worn Beauty'. For each of the **highlighted phrases/words**, note down what technique (using words in the **style list** above) you think the writer has used.

1. The photo was black and white, but I could still recognise her **smooth, brown** skin and youthful eyes. They looked **like warm pools of hot chocolate.**

2. Her brown-black hair was shiny, full of life. The **healthy mane** framed her delicate skin.

3. I am sharply reminded of reality as I hear the familiar **click clacking** of my Nana's worn slippers.

4. Nana's skin is rough and worn, **like the leather on a pair of old, tough boots**.

5. Years of hard work and now old age, have contributed to make a seemingly **shrunken, hunched** woman.

Task 5

Use the topic you chose for **Task 1**.

Make a list of the techniques from the style list that you would like to try and use in your writing. (You can use each technique more than once.)

Make notes on what details you could describe, using that technique and how you could describe them. (Two examples are given.)

Technique	Detail	Draft
Carefully chosen verb	The way Nana sits down in her chair	She **collapses** into her arm chair.
Simile	Her wrinkles	Deep wrinkles line her face **like small crevasses**.

Skill 3 – Structure (Organisation)

Each paragraph develops an idea or a detail; ideas are connected

(A): **Structure** material in a way that is **appropriate** to audience, purpose and text type.

(M): Structure material **clearly** in a way that is appropriate to audience, purpose and text type.

(E): Structure material clearly and **effectively** in a way that is appropriate to audience, purpose and text type.

Organisation of ideas suits requirements of the task

Sentences and paragraphs logically connect to make it easier for the reader to follow the ideas

Organisation and connections succeed all the way through; writing is tightly structured, with an effective, linked conclusion

6 English Achievement Standard 1.1

Organising the ideas is very important. Before you start writing, you should have a general outline of where you are going to start, the order of the ideas and various details, and where you will finish.

You need to look closely at your brainstorm and work out the most logical order for the ideas and details you wish to include. This forms the basis of your paragraphs. You might find you change this order on your second draft, but it provides a logical starting point for your work.

Example topic (Grandmother)

Order	Idea/detail
1	• Start with looking at Nana's old wedding photo • Describe looks
2	• Describe sense of personality from photograph
3	• Focus on present • Describe Nana walking towards me
4	• Describe how she looks now
5	• Focus on how old age has changed her
6	• Finish by quick comparison / link to myself (my age)

Task 6

Use the topic you chose in **Task 1**.

Think about where you want to start and finish your piece of writing and how to best order the idea/detail in-between. Complete the table below. (You may need more or fewer boxes than those provided.)

Order	Idea/detail
1	
2	
3	
4	
5	
6	

Skill 4 – Accuracy (writing conventions)

Errors of such frequency and level they detract from the reader's ability to read fluently, understand and enjoy the piece

Spelling, punctuation, grammar, etc

(A): Use **writing conventions** without **intrusive errors**.

(M) and (E): Use writing conventions **accurately**.

Very few errors, which do not spoil the reader's understanding or enjoyment

© ESA Publications (NZ) Ltd, Freephone 0800-372 266

Spelling mistakes, errors in punctuation and problems with sentence structure will prevent you from gaining 'Achieved' in this Standard; you must build in the time to read your work closely to reduce these errors.

Your teacher is allowed to check your draft work and they can note in the margin which lines have spelling errors in them, which lines have punctuation problems, sentence structure problems, etc – use this assistance to help you.

Strategies for poor spellers

Read over your work every couple of paragraphs:

- Circle any word you are not 100% sure about.
- Check each word in the dictionary (think about the initial sound the word makes to know where to start looking in the dictionary).
- If you can't find the word in the dictionary, choose another word!

Look closely for commonly confused words, such as:

- to, two and too;
- their, there and they're; etc.

Strategies if you have a weakness with punctuation

Possessive apostrophe, punctuation around direct speech, contractions, capital letters and the use of the comma can result in errors:

- Circle any piece of punctuation you are not 100% sure about.
- Refer to your classroom notes / ESA Year 11 English Study Guide punctuation section, to revise your area of weakness.

Strategies if you have problems with controlling sentences

Read your piece of writing 'aloud in your head'. If you are struggling for breath, the sentences are too long – look for somewhere to add commas or break the sentence into 2 or 3 sentences.

Check that each new sentence starts with a capital letter.

Task 7

This is based upon the Example topic (Grandmother).

Below are the first two paragraphs of a finished piece of writing, *The Worn Beauty*, by a Year 11 student. Certain errors are still present. Test your proofreading skills to see if you can find:

1. Three spelling mistakes.
2. Three punctuation errors.

> I picked up the faded, creased photo and an almost unreconisable face looked back at me. It was my Nana almost sixty years ago, at her wedding. The photo was black and white, but I could still recognise her smooth, brown skin and youthful eyes. They looked like warm pools of hot chocolate. She proudly stood upright, flashing her brilliant white teeth. Her strong figure held me mesmerised and a small smile spread across my face. Her black-brown hair was shiny, full of life. Not a single strand stood out of place. The healthy mane framed her delicate skin. The smoothness' of her skin reminded me of a perfectly-new brown paper bag, like the ones that sit on the bench of a bakery.
>
> She looked astounding. At a mere 19-years-old, not many people wouldnt, but she had something special. Nana had a glowing radience that beamed out from every inch of her body. She looked so sure of herself able and agile with a commanding, yet calming aura, all at the same time. Although she was comitting the rest of her life to the man whom she loved, you could still recognise a sense of independence coming from deep within her.

8 English Achievement Standard 1.1

Task 8

1. Using the notes you have made on the topic of your choice:
   - Write the first draft.
   - Look closely at your description and detail, add/alter certain techniques.
   - Proofread your work closely, looking for spelling errors, punctuation problems and weakness with sentence structure.

Continue on your own paper if necessary.

Produce formal writing

NCEA Achievement Standard 1.2
Externally assessed
3 credits

Achievement standard 1.2 focuses on four main skill areas – your ability to:
- Develop ideas.
- Write in a clear, concise manner.
- Structure material effectively.
- Proofread your work for accuracy in spelling, punctuation and grammar.

The end-of-year examination will offer a range of topics. You are required to select one and produce a written argument that explores the topic. You must write in excess of 250 words.

You should spend 45 minutes on the question. Approximately 20 minutes of this time should be spent on completing a detailed brainstorm and/or draft.

Your finished piece of formal writing should express ideas, information and/or opinions that are explained and supported by examples. It should be logically organised using an appropriate structure, and use acceptable spelling, punctuation and grammar.

Assessment criteria

Achieved	Merit	Excellence
Express **idea(s)** with supporting detail in a piece of formal writing.	*Develop* **idea(s)** with supporting detail *and explanation* in a piece of formal writing.	*Develop* **idea(s)** *convincingly* with supporting detail and explanation in a piece of formal writing.
Use a writing **style** appropriate to audience, purpose and text type.	Use a *controlled* writing **style** appropriate to audience, purpose and text type.	Use a controlled writing **style** appropriate to audience, purpose and text type, *and which commands attention*.
Structure material in a way that is appropriate to audience, purpose and text type.	**Structure** material *clearly* in a way that is appropriate to audience, purpose and text type.	**Structure** material clearly *and effectively* in a way that is appropriate to audience, purpose and text type.
Use **writing conventions** without intrusive errors.	Use **writing conventions** without intrusive errors.	Use **writing conventions** *accurately*.

Skill 1 – Ideas

Ideas may be based on facts or information, and can include opinions, observations, and arguments.

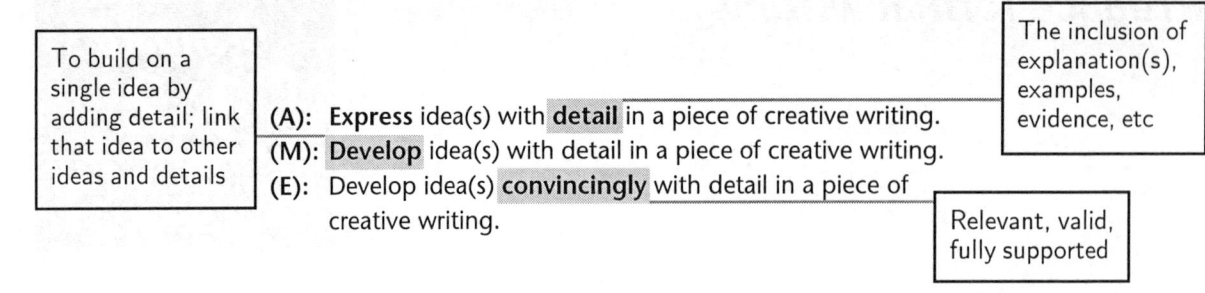

To build on a single idea by adding detail; link that idea to other ideas and details	**(A):** **Express** idea(s) with **detail** in a piece of creative writing. **(M):** **Develop** idea(s) with detail in a piece of creative writing. **(E):** Develop idea(s) **convincingly** with detail in a piece of creative writing.	The inclusion of explanation(s), examples, evidence, etc
		Relevant, valid, fully supported

When selecting a topic in the examination it is very important that you choose a topic you have knowledge of and opinions on. The ideas that you communicate form the heart of your writing and you must be clear about your purpose and audience before beginning your answer.

Step 1: Brainstorm key ideas, facts, information, opinions and/or observations

It is essential to make sure everything is relevant to the topic – it is sometimes helpful to do this by using a 'spider diagram'.

> The Example topic **'Technology and change'** will be used throughout this chapter.

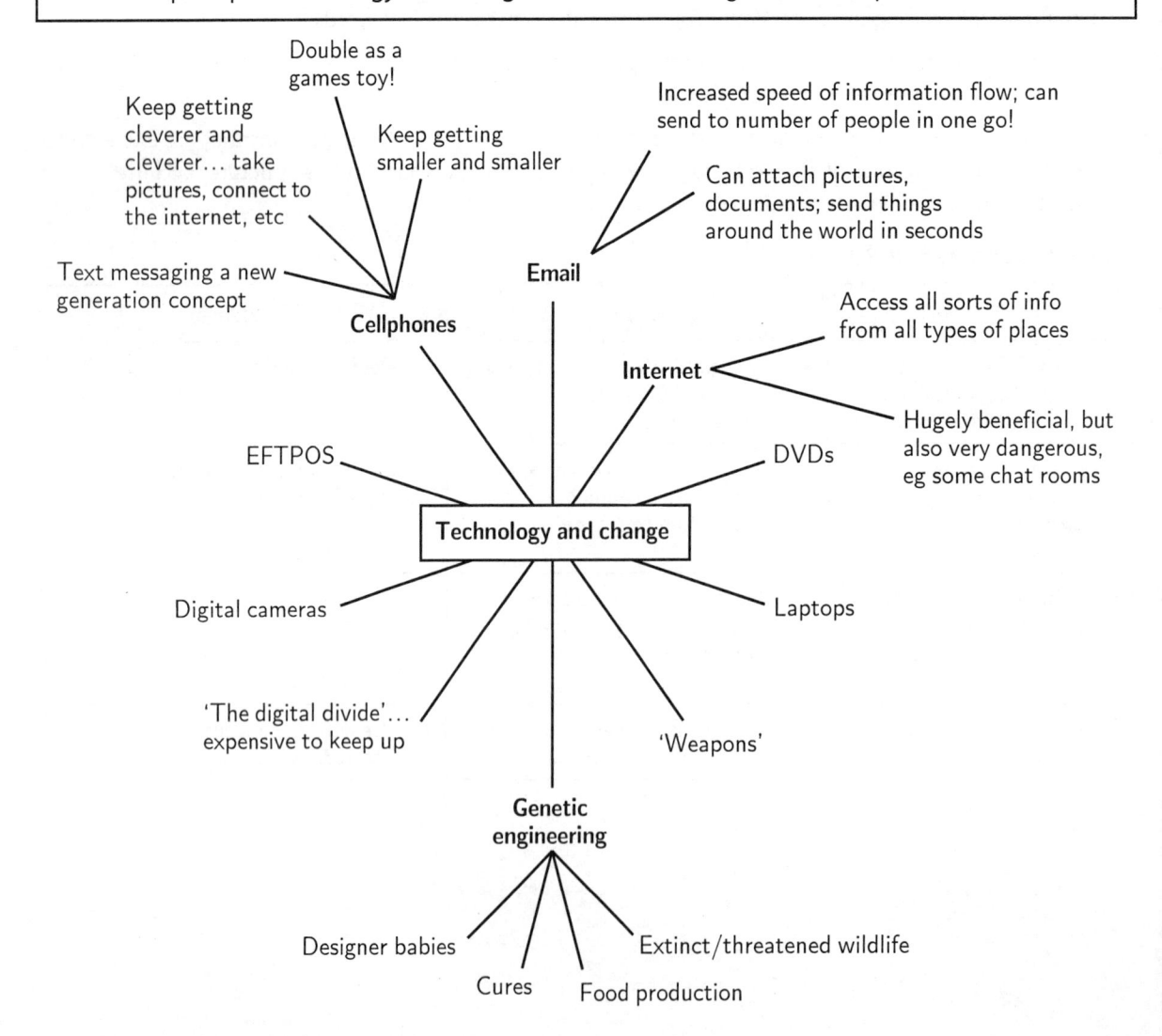

Cellphones
- Keep getting cleverer and cleverer... take pictures, connect to the internet, etc
- Text messaging a new generation concept
- Double as a games toy!
- Keep getting smaller and smaller

Email
- Increased speed of information flow; can send to number of people in one go!
- Can attach pictures, documents; send things around the world in seconds

Internet
- Access all sorts of info from all types of places
- Hugely beneficial, but also very dangerous, eg some chat rooms

Technology and change connects to: EFTPOS, DVDs, Digital cameras, Laptops, 'The digital divide'... expensive to keep up, 'Weapons', Genetic engineering

Genetic engineering
- Designer babies
- Cures
- Food production
- Extinct/threatened wildlife

Task 1

Complete a brainstorm 'spider diagram' similar to that on the previous page but use the topic 'Modern youth has too much temptation.'

> Modern youth has too much temptation

Step 2: Decide the *purpose* of your piece of writing

What is your overall message going to be? Use your initial brainstorm to do this.

The *purpose* can fall into a range of categories, such as:
- Trying to persuade the reader of something.
- Offering a balance of opinions.
- Offering suggestions.

The Example topic (Technology and change) could have the following range of purposes:
- Technology is changing too rapidly and is designed to leave us behind.
- Technology has a life of its own and is growing and changing daily.
- Technology offers wonderful opportunities.
- Technology offers both benefits and risks.

Task 2

Using your brainstorm from **Task 1** on 'Modern youth has too much temptation', decide what the specific purpose of your piece of writing will be.

Purpose / focus of my writing: _____

_____

_____

Step 3: Brainstorm how to develop key ideas of your writing

For each of the key areas, think about how you will build on the idea/develop it, what detail you could add, what examples/facts you can use, etc.

The following is based upon the Example topic (Technology and change).

Idea / key area	Development and details
Benefits of increased food production worldwide.	• World population increasing by 1 billion every 20 years. • 3 billion people live in poverty. • GM could produce a faster growing wheat. • Financial gain from GM to farmers.
Potential threat of 'designer babies'.	• IQ, looks, special abilities, etc, decided before birth. • Threatens our uniqueness. • We could 'play God' in terms of what we choose to alter/ modify… eg height.
Etc.	

Task 3

Using your spider diagram from **Task 1**, group your ideas into 4 or 5 key areas of discussion (ie the most important points that need to be raised).

Brainstorm how you will **develop** your key ideas for 'Modern youth has too much temptation'.

Think carefully about how you will build on each idea, what detail you could add, what examples/facts you can use, etc.

Idea / key area	Development and details

Skill 2 – Style

> The writing must suit the requirements of the task, eg a business letter should be formal with no slang

> Must think carefully about your expression, use of language, tone, etc

(A): Use a writing style **appropriate** to audience, purpose and text type.
(M): Use a **controlled** writing style appropriate to audience, purpose and text type.
(E): Use a controlled writing style appropriate to audience, purpose and text type, and which **commands attention**.

> Extensive vocabulary range, variety of sentence structures – shows a flair for language; makes the reader want to read it

The **style** of your writing is something you should work on, draft, reshape and continue to change until your writing shows control and crafting.

It is important that your writing is formal in tone – this is not a casual letter to a friend; you want the reader to take your ideas seriously. You want the marker to be impressed by your quality of thought and clear, correct expression.

With style, you should think about:
- The purpose and audience for your piece of writing.
- The clarity of your sentence structure and incorporation of a variety of sentence types and lengths.
- Using a broad range of vocabulary – looking to use complex vocabulary.

Task 4

Read the following introductory paragraph on the Example topic (Technology and change). The style of this paragraph 'needs work'. In particular, look at how you might improve on the casual language, vocabulary choice, grammar and sentence structure. Note what you would change and how you would change it.

> Genetic engineering is really important at the moment but over the past 20 years, computers, cell phones and other gizmos have been more important. Now a days though scientists are into genetic engineering. Because of GM more food could be made and dead or nearly dead species brought back to life and cures could be made for stuff we can't cure now and flash 'designer babies' could be created. There are good things that we could get from genetic engineering but heaps of bad things too.

Skill 3 – Structure (organisation)

Use a new paragraph for each idea; use an introduction and conclusion

(A): **Structure** material in a way that is **appropriate** to audience, purpose and text type.
(M): Structure material **clearly** in a way that is appropriate to audience, purpose and text type.
(E): Structure material clearly and **effectively** in a way that is appropriate to audience, purpose and text type.

Organisation of ideas suits requirements of the task

Sentences and paragraphs logically connect to make it easier for the reader to follow your ideas

Organisation and connections succeed all the way through; writing is tightly structured, with an effective linked conclusion

The way you organise your ideas is very important. Your piece of writing should be approximately 6 or 7 paragraphs in length and be structured in the following way:

- Paragraph 1 – Introduction to the purpose and topic of your piece of writing.
- Paragraph 2 – Idea/key area number 1, fully explained and backed up with relevant examples and facts.
- Paragraph 3 – Idea/key area number 2, fully explained and backed up with relevant examples and facts.
- Paragraph 4 – Idea/ key area number 3, fully explained and backed up with relevant examples and facts.
- Paragraph 5 – Idea/key area number 4, fully explained and backed up with relevant examples and facts.
- Paragraph 6 – Conclusion that summarises your opinion on the topic.

Step 1: Order your ideas/key areas of discussion

Refer to your key areas brainstorm (from **Task 3**) – consider the areas of discussion carefully and put the ideas into a logical order.

Example topic (Technology and change):

Paragraph 1	Introduction.
Paragraph 2	Potential to increase the world food supply and aid the fight against world poverty.
Paragraph 3	Potential cures for currently incurable diseases.
Paragraph 4	Positives and negatives of impact on extinct/threatened wildlife species.
Paragraph 5	Threat of 'designer babies'.
Paragraph 6	Conclusion.

Task 5

Continue with the topic 'Modern youth has too much temptation.' Referring to your earlier brainstorms (especially **Task 3**), plan the order of your ideas/key areas of discussion.

Paragraph 1	Introduction.
Paragraph 2	
Paragraph 3	
Paragraph 4	
Paragraph 5	
Paragraph 6	

Step 2: Focus each paragraph around a particular point and develop it

It is useful to apply the **PDR paragraph structure** to your formal writing.

The PDR paragraph structure

A paragraph should be focused, coherent, and well developed. Paragraphs are unified around a main point, and all sentences in the paragraph should clearly relate to that point in some way. The paragraph's main idea should be supported with specific information that develops or discusses the main idea in greater detail.

Each new paragraph should begin with a clear point **(P)**. This point should then be followed by appropriate development **(D)** and specific reference to examples, facts, etc **(R)**.

P = **P**oint is made – a single sentence which sets up the focus of the paragraph.

D = **D**evelop the point – explain clearly what you mean in 2 or 3 sentences.

R = **R**efer to a specific example, fact, known opinion, etc.

Example topic (Technology and change) forms the basis for the model following.

Introduces focus of genetic engineering and outlines what the essay will cover	Genetic engineering is leading the way in the advancement of technology. Over the past 20 years, computers, cellphones and other information technology, such as the internet, have dominated the limelight of technology development. However, scientists in the 21st century are now focusing on new discoveries in the field of genetic engineering. Through genetic modification more food could be produced, endangered species protected and extinct species recreated, cures for currently incurable diseases found, or designer babies created. Whilst there are potentially great benefits to be gained from genetic engineering, many people in society consider the risks outweigh the benefits.
Point is in **bold**	**One of the major benefits of genetic modification is that food production could be increased.** *The world population is increasing by 1 billion people every 20 years.* *With 3 billion already living in poverty*, it would be beneficial to all people worldwide if more food could be produced and distributed evenly, with relation to the population in each country. *In the future, scientists could use genetic modification to produce wheat plants which would grow at twice or even three times the normal rate. If in the poorer countries twice as much wheat could be harvested in one season, many of the people who live in poverty, would have more to eat. This would be a huge benefit to farmers, who would have more to sell and export, resulting in a financial gain.*
Refer is in **bold and italics**	
Development of the point is in *italics*	

Cures for present-day incurable diseases could also be discovered through genetic modifications, increasing the average life expectancy. *Worldwide, people suffer from genetic diseases such as cystic fibrosis, and various cancers. Some of these diseases are fatal. A large percentage of people who suffer from cystic fibrosis and many leukaemia cancer sufferers are children. Scientists are researching remedies through genetic modification to try and cure or prevent these diseases.*

There are also many transmissible diseases, such as AIDS (caused by the HIV virus). ***AIDS is considered to be one of the most dangerous viruses known to humankind.*** *Scientists have found it difficult to discover a cure for AIDS because the HIV virus continually changes its genetic make-up. If a cure could be found through genetic engineering, the millions of people with HIV could be prevented from developing full-blown AIDS.*

16 English Achievement Standard 1.2

Skill 4 – Accuracy (writing conventions)

Spelling, punctuation, grammar, etc

(A) and (M): Use **writing conventions** without **intrusive errors**.
(E): Use writing conventions **accurately**.

Errors of such frequency and level that they detract from the reader's ability to read fluently, understand and enjoy the piece

Very few errors, which do not spoil the reader's understanding or enjoyment

Spelling mistakes, errors in punctuation and problems with sentence structure will prevent an 'Achieved' grade being awarded – build in the time to read your work closely to eliminate these types of errors.

Strategies for poor spellers
- Complete as many practice topics as possible before the examination. From each piece of writing, create a spelling list of words related to that topic that you need to memorise.
- Create a spelling list of words regularly used in formal writing, such as 'nevertheless', 'considered', 'public opinion', etc (create this list using your practice essays as well).
- When writing, sound out difficult words that you are uncertain about – if you remain unsure if the spelling is correct, select a different word.
- Read over your work every couple of paragraphs – look closely for commonly confused words such as to, two and too; their, there and they're; etc.

Strategies for a weakness with punctuation
Learn about the rules and practise the area(s) of punctuation you tend to 'trip up on'.

In the exam, make a conscious effort to focus on these areas, and take your time ensuring you apply the rules you have learnt.

Strategies if you have problems with controlling sentences
- Read your piece of writing 'aloud in your head'. If you are struggling for breath, the sentences are too long – look for somewhere to add commas or break the sentence into 2 or 3 sentences.
- Check that each new sentence starts with a capital letter.

Task 6

Test your proofreading skills on the final three paragraphs of the example topic (Technology and change). Identify (by circling):
- Three spelling mistakes.
- Three punctuation errors.

(The text is in the form **P = bold**, *D = italics* and ***R = bold and italics***.)

> **There are obvious benifits, but also potential risks, involved with recreating extinct animal species.** *Through genetic modification it could become possible once more for all creatures to walk the earth. Animals such as mammoths, moas and dinosaurs would no longer be just skeletons in museums or fairytale creatures in books. Scientists' could also prevent endangered species from becoming extinct. However, the world population is steadily increasing and if each animal species became as common as possums are in New Zealand, there is a decided threat to resources.* ***Through genetic modification scientists could bring dinosors to the 21st century. 'Jurassic Park' could become fact instead of fiction.***
>
> **Another risk to society is that scientists could use genetic modification to create 'designer' babies.** *As humankind we were all born individuals. If these babies were created it would be an unatural acceleration of evolution. Parents could choose looks and qualities for their children and two people could be*

born identical, right down to their fingerprints. Before they were born, a babys characteristics, IQ or sporting ability could be enhanced. Everyone could excel at everything they did. We would suffer a loss of identity and uniqueness. **A 2.4 m child could be the product of parents whose wish was for their child to become a professional basketball player, the best in the world.**

Whether it is producing more food, curing 'incurable diseases' creating designer babies or recreating extinct animal species, many benefits and risks are involved in genetic modification. Although the effects of genetic engineering may not have an immediate impact on society, it is destined to have a major influence on future generations. Technology is, and always will be changing.

Task 7

Using the notes (**Tasks 2**, **3** and **5**) you have made so far on the topic 'Modern youth has too much temptation':

- Write the first draft in the space provided below. (You will no doubt need more paper – continue on refill.)
- Look closely at each paragraph.
  Does the first sentence clearly summarise the **P**oint of the paragraph?
  Have you **D**eveloped the point – ie clearly explained what you mean in a way the reader can follow?
  Have you **R**eferred to examples/facts, etc?

Proofread your work closely, looking for spelling errors, punctuation problems and weaknesses with sentence structure.

Write your first draft on the lines below.

Current events – Questions for Practice

Formal writing questions are often topical. You should read broadly on current events to ensure you have relevant ideas and information that you could use. You should read the daily newspapers, watch/listen to The News, read magazines such as *The Listener, North and South*, etc.

Current issues that could feature in 1.2 exam questions for 2003 could include:
- Dog controls are essential for public safety.
- We have become immune to war and terrorism.
- The texting generation.
- There should be more New Zealand content on television.
- The international year of water.
- We waste electricity in our daily lives.

Produce formal writing **19**

NCEA Level 1 Questions

In the exam you will be provided with four pages of ruled lines for writing your answer to the Achievement Standard 1.2 question.
You should practise all of the topics below – however, you only have to write on *one* in the exam.
Use your own paper to answer each question.

1. Learning another language is a great thing.
2. Winning is the most important thing.
3. Fast food is bad for your health.
4. Extreme sports are the future of sport.
5. A good teacher cares.
6. Young people waste too much time with TV and video games.

7. Living in the country is better than living in the city.

8. New Zealanders do not know their history.

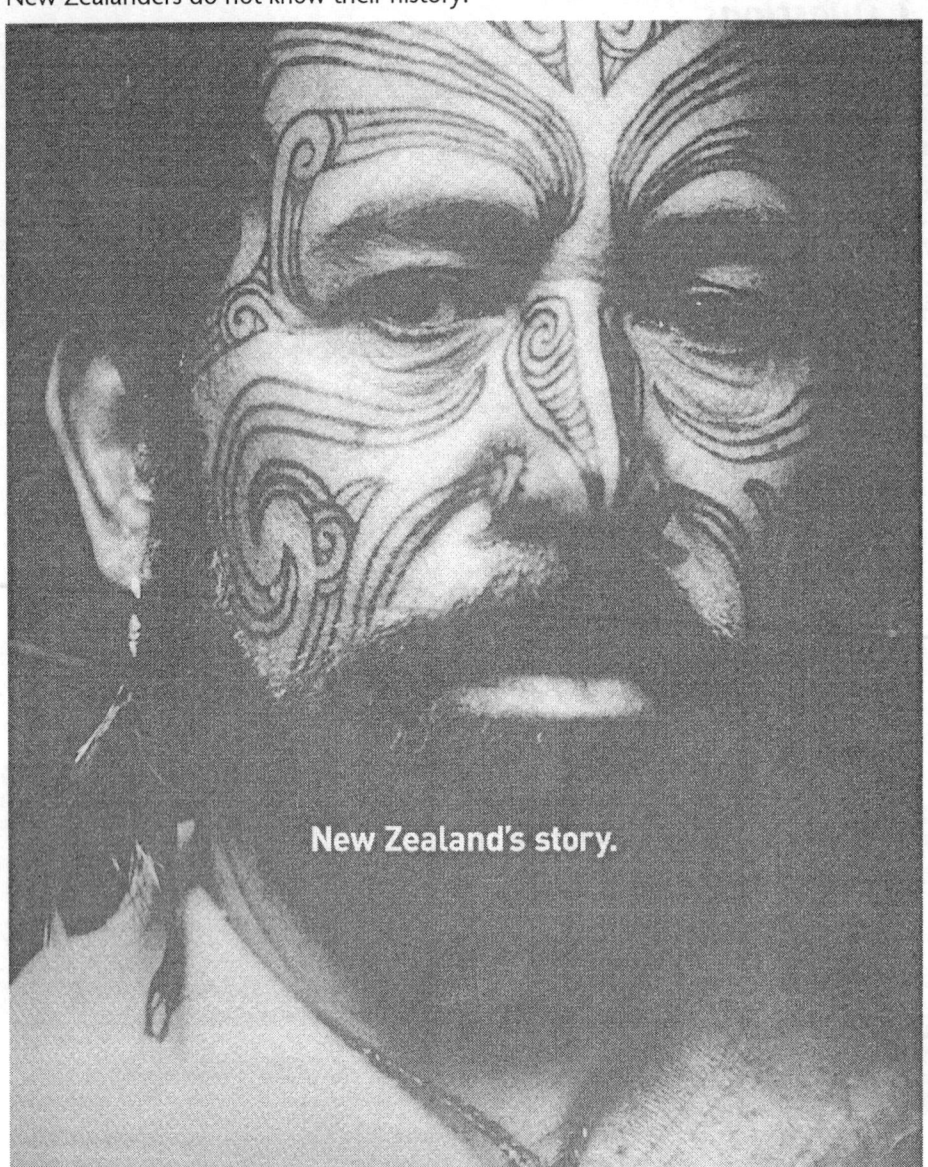

New Zealand's story.

Read, study and understand an extended written text

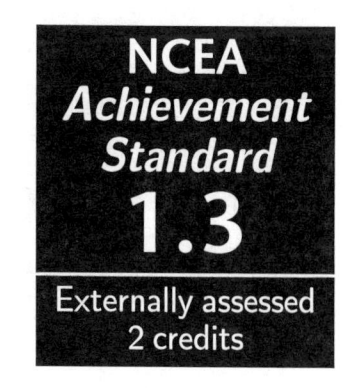

NCEA Achievement Standard 1.3
Externally assessed
2 credits

Achievement Standard 1.3 assesses your understanding of, and response to, an extended written text.

Extended written texts include Novel, Non-fiction, Extended hyperfiction and Drama script.

You will be required to write approximately 200 words in response to one of the questions offered in the external Achievement Standard examination – it may be necessary to write more than this to achieve 'Merit' or 'Excellence'.

You should spend approximately 25 minutes on answering the question.

- Answer all parts of the question.
- Use clear, well-chosen points.
- Back up your points with relevant reference to the moments/events from the text.

Assessment criteria

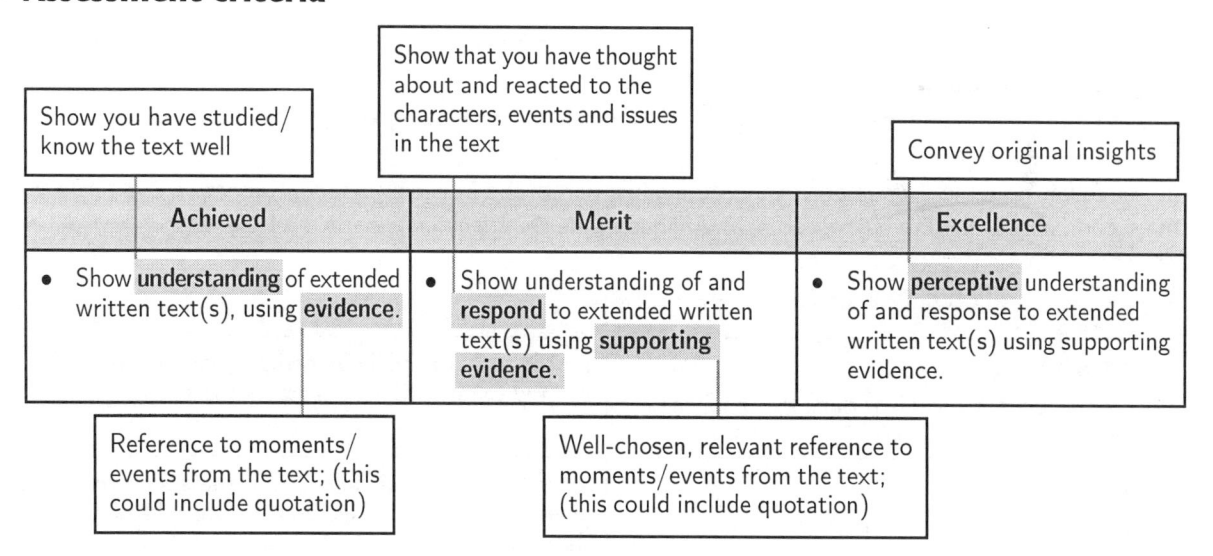

Show you have studied/know the text well

Show that you have thought about and reacted to the characters, events and issues in the text

Convey original insights

Achieved	Merit	Excellence
• Show **understanding** of extended written text(s), using **evidence**.	• Show understanding of and **respond** to extended written text(s) using **supporting evidence**.	• Show **perceptive** understanding of and response to extended written text(s) using supporting evidence.

Reference to moments/events from the text; (this could include quotation)

Well-chosen, relevant reference to moments/events from the text; (this could include quotation)

Types of questions

Questions on an extended written text largely fall into five main categories:

Question category	Examples
Character	• How a character changes, grows • Character relationships • An important character • What a character learns • The challenges a character faces • Character conflict

Theme	• The main idea(s) of the text (message or issue) • Key moments that raise an important theme • What you are encouraged to think about
Plot	• The relevance of the beginning • An important moment/ event • The climax • The effectiveness of the conclusion
Setting	• Time • Place • Social environment • The impact on characters, events, etc
Style	• The effective use of language • Literary devices, such as figurative language • Narrative voice

Formula for success – structuring your answer

Step 1: Think about *The Question*

Look closely at the question. Look at the key words and decide how many parts the question has.

Example question	Question analysis
'Describe the most important thing that happened to a main character in your text and explain, with detailed reasons, why it was important.'	This question has two parts: • Describe the most important thing that happened to the character. • Explain why it was important.

Step 2: Think about *The Ideas*

Aim to write 4 or 5 paragraphs – brainstorm what the focus of each paragraph will be and make specific notes related to your text.

(In the following table, *Paragraph 1* relates to the first part of the *Example question*, *Paragraphs 2–4* relate to the second part of the *Example question*, as outlined in the *Question analysis* above.)

Focus of paragraph	Example brainstorm using the text, *Krystyna's Story*, by Halina Ogonowska-Coates
Paragraph 1 Describe the most important thing that happened to the character	Forced to leave childhood home. Given ½ hour, only allowed to take 100 kg of possessions.
Paragraph 2 Explain the 1st reason why this is important	It changes her emotionally. She witnesses death, cruelty, deprivation (Ciepluski + camp); brother and sister die at the camp.
Paragraph 3 Explain the 2nd reason why this is important	Her resulting journey, in particular her journey across USSR (she ends up alone), forced to steal, etc.
Paragraph 4 Explain a 3rd reason why this is important	She settles in New Zealand.

Read, study and understand an extended written text

Step 3: Think about *The Structure* of your Answer
Write your answer using the PDR structure.

The PDR paragraph structure

A paragraph should be focused, coherent, and well developed. Paragraphs are unified around a main point, and all sentences in the paragraph should clearly relate to that point in some way. The paragraph's main idea should be supported with specific information that develops or discusses the main idea in greater detail.

Each new paragraph should begin with a clear point **(P)**. This point should then be followed by appropriate development **(D)** and specific reference to the text **(R)**.

P = **P**oint is made – a single sentence which sets up the focus of the paragraph.

D = **D**evelop the point – explain clearly what you mean in 2 or 3 sentences.

R = **R**efer to a specific moment/ event/ conversation/ quotation from the text.

Using the PDR structure

Example question:

'Describe the most important thing that happened to a main character in your text and explain, with detailed reasons, why it was important.'

Paragraph 1: description of the most important thing that happened to the main character.	**The most important thing that happened to the main character of Krystyna in *Krystyna's Story*, by Halina Ogonowska-Coates, was her forced removal from the family home in Baranowiczie and the resulting journeys, ultimately leading her to a new home on the other side of the world.** Krystyna and her family were a farming family and the land was their livelihood. Krystyna has fond memories of her life before the war and comments, "It was a happy childhood." However, on September 1st 1939 Poland was attacked by both Russia and Germany. Krystyna and her family are forcibly removed from their home in Poland by occupying Russian soldiers and Krystyna's life is changed forever. The Russian soldiers initially vandalise Krystyna's home and later they attack the family physically, kicking Mama repeatedly with their heavy boots. Finally they are given 30 minutes to pack up 100 kilos of their possessions and leave their house for good. At first, this action is important to the book because it helps to form the scene, setting, attitude and atmosphere of the book. Without her removal, Krystyna would not have a story to tell.
Point is in **bold**	**This event is so important to the book because it leads to Krystyna's emotional experiences that change her personality and outlook on life.** *Once she is forced from her home she is taken to a Russian labour camp. She suffers cruelty, misunderstanding and deprivation at the hands of the Russian soldiers on her journey on the ciepluszki, and later in the camp itself.* ***Whilst on the cattle wagon (ciepluski) she has to survive on a portion of bread each day. There is no room to lie down and lice and disease fill the wagon. She witnesses people dying, bodies being thrown from the wagon and cold-blooded murder. The camp is not much better. She must fulfil a set quota of work each day if she is to eat.*** *As a result she consequently changes from a bright, bubbly and innocent child to a depressed and broken person who is made to grow up too fast. This all starts with her removal from her home, and continues during the following journeys.*
Development of the point is in *italics*	
Refer is in ***bold and italics***	

Another reason her removal from her home is so important to the book is the events that result from it. The most important of these is her journey through the USSR by herself after her family has died. *This part of the book is like a turning point, a bridge between her time in Europe and her coming time in New Zealand. Without her removal, these travels would not have happened.* **Krystyna and the other survivors of the camp are eventually released. She walks out of the camp with only her mother and her aunt. Her mother dies quite soon after and her aunt is left behind. Krystyna learns to steal to survive and is forced to look after herself. She is alone in the world. When she arrives at the orphanage in Teheran, and later, in New Zealand, Krystyna is trying to start a new life to replace her old one in Baranowiczie.**

The final reason that Krystyna's removal from her childhood home is so important is that it brings her to New Zealand – a new life, along with a new culture. *It is because she is forced from her home that night that her own family are destined to grow up as New Zealanders. It is ironic, however, that what seems to be the simplest part of her long journey, turns out to be as challenging and upsetting as her earlier experiences.* **Krystyna attends school in New Zealand and again faces deprivation; she is not allowed to speak Polish, is forced to clean and do laundry for her board and is not allowed to return 'home' to the Pahiatua camp during the holidays. Eventually, however, Krystyna settles at the Polish hostel in Lyall Bay, Wellington; she finds the new home she has been searching for since the night she was ordered to leave her family home. "Here was a place where I belonged, with people who had become my family in New Zealand."**

Task 1
Using a PDR template
Using the text you have studied in class, answer the same question as modelled above. Follow the structure and guidance given by the template.

Question:

'Describe the most important thing that happened to a main character in your text and explain, with detailed reasons, why it was important.'

> The answer template is set out in the following manner:
> - **PDR** is indicated by **P**oint, **D**evelop and **R**efer.
> - The beginning of each paragraph has been started for you; this is in **bold**.
> - The text in *italics* is guidance on how to continue, what to add, etc.

In the text, *(title)* _____ **, by** *(author)* _____ ,

a main character is *(name a main character)* _____ .

(**P**oint) **The most important thing that happens to** *(name of character)* _____
(summarise the 'most important thing that happens to your chosen character', in one sentence)

is _____

_____

(**D**evelop *this sentence with a full description of the event/happening and* **R**efer *to specific moments/details from the text)*

(**P**oint) **This is important because**

(**D**evelop further what you mean and **R**efer to specific moments/details from the text)

(**P**oint) **It is also important because**

(**D**evelop further what you mean and **R**efer to specific moments/details from the text)

(**P**oint) **Finally, it is also important because**

(**D**evelop further what you mean and **R**efer to specific moments/details from the text)

Answering Plot Questions

The plot means what happens in a story, and why it happens. Novels and drama scripts all have plots. Since a plot is something made up, a non-fiction work does not really have a plot; but you can write about the events the text describes.

The main events typically start with a brief 'set up' period where important characters are introduced, details of the setting are established, etc. The story then gets underway with the introduction of the 'catalyst', an event that starts the tension mounting. The events then build to a climax, the point of highest tension in the story. This is typically followed by a short 'wind down' period, called the resolution or denouement.

Task 2

The plot of your text

Complete the graph below, by selecting and recording the main events of your text on the blank lines provided.

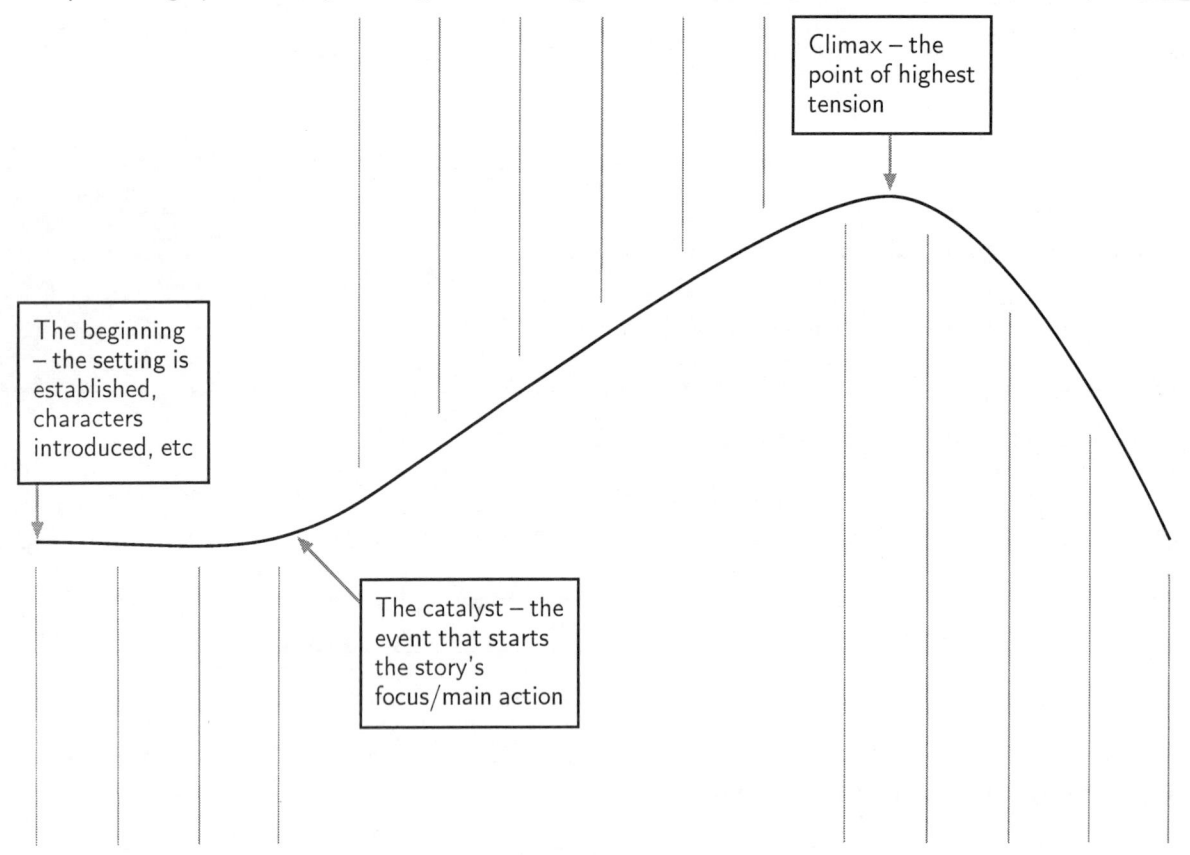

Climax – the point of highest tension

The beginning – the setting is established, characters introduced, etc

The catalyst – the event that starts the story's focus/main action

Task 3
NCEA Level 1 Question for 'the plot'
'Describe an important event in your text and explain why it is important.'

> A model answer is provided in the answer section for *Water in the Blood*, by Alan Bunn.

Step 1: Think about the question
This question has two parts:
- Describe an important event.
- Explain why it is important.

Step 2: Think about the ideas
Brainstorm the focus of your 4 (or 5) paragraphs.

General focus of paragraph	Specific focus using your text
Paragraph 1	
Paragraph 2	
Paragraph 3	
Paragraph 4	

Step 3: Using the PDR structure, write your own answer

Continue on your own paper if necessary.

Answering Character Questions

A **character** is a person (or sometimes an animal, ghost, etc) that appears in a text. If you are writing about a non-fiction work, remember that the characters have not been created by the author but are real people.

Texts generally have major characters and minor characters.
- Major characters are those that are central to the events and ideas of the story.
- Minor characters, whilst not the focus of the story, may contribute on a lesser scale to events and ideas.

Character questions can also explore character relationships, character change/growth, character action and reaction.

Task 4
The characters of your text
Consider the book you studied in class and fill in the boxes below. You may have to take up more room than is given.

Main characters in my text are:	Minor characters in my text are:
Important relationships in my text are:	Characters who grow or change in my text are:

Task 5
NCEA Level 1 Question for 'character'
'Describe the most important relationship in your text. Explain how this relationship influences events.'

> A model answer is provided in the answer section for *Spider*, by William Taylor.

Step 1: Think about the question
This question has two parts:
- Describe the most important relationship.
- Explain how the relationship influences events.

Step 2: Think about the ideas
Brainstorm the focus of your 4 (or 5) paragraphs:

Read, study and understand an extended written text 29

General focus of paragraph	Specific focus using your text
Paragraph 1	
Paragraph 2	
Paragraph 3	
Paragraph 4	

Step 3: Using the PDR structure, write your own answer

_____

_____

_____

_____

_____

_____

_____

_____

_____

_____

_____

_____

_____

_____

_____

_____ *Continue on your own paper if necessary.*

Answering Setting Questions

The **setting** is where events happen (place) and when they happen (time). It also includes the social conditions of the era/place. For example, if the book is set in Germany during World War Two, the social conditions would include wartime conditions such as rationing, black-outs, bombing, etc.

Questions typically focus on how the setting influences the events or affects the characters, etc.

Task 6

The setting of your text

Consider the book you studied in class and complete the table below. You may need less or more room than is given.

Place setting	Country	
	City/town	
	Important places where action happens (eg a school, a farm, etc)	
Time setting	Era/year	
Social setting	Things happening around that time	

Task 7

NCEA Level 1 Question for 'setting'

'Describe the setting of your text and explain, with detailed reasons, how this setting is important.'

> A model answer is provided in the answer section for *Goodnight Mister Tom*, by Michelle Magorian.

Step 1: Think about the question

This question has two parts:
- Describe the setting.
- Explain how it is important.

Step 2: Think about the ideas

Brainstorm the focus of your 4 (or 5) paragraphs:

General focus of paragraph	Specific focus using your text
Paragraph 1	
Paragraph 2	

Read, study and understand an extended written text **31**

Paragraph 3	
Paragraph 4	

Step 3: Using the PDR structure, write your own answer

_____
_____
_____
_____
_____
_____
_____
_____
_____
_____
_____
_____
_____
_____
_____
_____
_____
_____ *Continue on your own paper if necessary.*

Answering Theme Questions

The **theme** is the central idea of the text – the message(s) or issue(s) you are invited to think about while you are reading the text.

Themes generally emerge from the characters' actions and reactions. What they do, say and think about help us, the reader, focus on some important ideas that the author also wants us to think about.

Task 8
The theme of your text
Consider the book you studied in class and complete the table following. You may need less or more room than is given.

32 English Achievement Standard 1.3

Important ideas the reader is encouraged to think about in the text	Events/characters that encourage us to think about the idea
1.	
2.	
3.	

Task 9

NCEA Level 1 Question for 'theme'

'Explain an important idea in your text and give detailed reasons as to why it was important.'

> A model answer is provided in the answer section for *Looking for Alibrandi*, by Melina Marchetta.

Step 1: Think about the question

This question has two parts:
- Explain an important idea.
- Explain why the idea was important.

Step 2: Think about the ideas

Brainstorm the focus of your 4 (or 5) paragraphs:

General focus of paragraph	Specific focus using your text
Paragraph 1	
Paragraph 2	
Paragraph 3	
Paragraph 4	

Step 3: Using the PDR structure, write your own answer

_____

Continue on your own paper if necessary.

Task 10

NCEA Level 1 Question for 'general questions'

General questions, like the one following, allow you to discuss a range of aspects of the text – plot, character, setting, themes, etc – all in one answer.

'Explain, with detailed examples, why you thought your text was worth reading.'

> A model answer is provided in the answer section for *Spider*, by William Taylor.

Step 1: Think about the question

This question has only one part:
- Explain why the text was worth studying.

Step 2: Think about the ideas

Brainstorm the focus of your 4 (or 5) paragraphs:

General focus of paragraph	Specific focus using your text
Paragraph 1	
Paragraph 2	
Paragraph 3	
Paragraph 4	

Step 3: Using the PDR structure, write your own answer

Continue on your own paper if necessary.

NCEA Level 1 Questions

> In the exam you will be provided with five pages of ruled lines for writing your answer for the Achievement Standard 1.3 question.
>
> You should practise all of the topics below – however, you only have to write on one in the exam.
>
> Use your own paper to answer each question.

1. Describe an **idea** that **interested** you in the text.
   Explain **why** this **idea interested** you.

2. Describe an **important place or period (time)** in the text.
   Explain **why** it was **important**.

3. Describe an **important relationship** in the text.
   Explain **why** the relationship was **important**.

4. Describe a **challenge faced by a character** in the text.
   Explain **how** the character **dealt with** the challenge.

5. Describe an **important incident** in the text.
   Explain **how** it **affected** an **important character**.

6. Describe an **interesting aspect of the text's style***.
   Explain **why** it was **interesting**.

   * This could include word choice, use of language, the structure or layout of the text, and any other interesting techniques the writer has used.

Read, study and understand a number of short written texts

NCEA Achievement Standard 1.4
Externally assessed
2 credits

Achievement Standard 1.4 assesses your understanding of, and response to, at least two short written texts of the same genre (ie two short texts of the same type – for example, two poems, or two short stories).

Short written texts include Short story, Poetry, Short hyperfiction and Print media.

You will be required to write approximately 200 words in response to one of the questions offered in the external Achievement Standards examination – it may be necessary to write more than this to achieve 'Merit' or 'Excellence', as you must write about two texts in detail.

You may choose to use two texts by the same author, but you do not have to.

You should spend approximately 25 minutes on answering the question.

- Answer all parts of the question.
- Refer to at least two texts of the same type within the answer.
- Use clear, well chosen points.
- Back up your points with relevant reference to the moments/events from each text.

Assessment criteria

Show you have studied/know the texts well

Show that you have thought about, and reacted to, the characters, events and issues in each text

Convey original insights

Achieved	Merit	Excellence
• Show **understanding** of at least two short written texts of the **same genre**, using **evidence**.	• Show understanding of and **respond to** at least two short written texts of the same genre using **supporting evidence**.	• Show **perceptive** understanding of and response to at least two short written texts of the same genre using supporting evidence.

The same type of text, eg two poems

Reference to moments/events from each text (this could include quotation)

Well-chosen, relevant reference to moments/events from each text (this could include quotation)

Types of questions

The various types of 'short written texts' are quite distinctive – a short story typically has a tightly constructed plot, poetry often has no plot at all; poetry and print media won't necessarily have characters.

Therefore, it is particularly important to pick a question that suits your specific texts.

Question category	Examples
Character	• How a character changes, grows • Character relationships • An important character • What a character learns • The challenges a character faces • Character conflict
Theme	• The main idea(s) of the text (message or issue) • Key moments that raise an important theme • What you are encouraged to think about
Plot	• The relevance of the beginning • An important moment/event • The climax • The effectiveness of the conclusion
Setting	• Time • Place • Social environment • The impact on characters, events, etc
Style	• The effective use of language • Literary devices, such as figurative language • Narrative voice

Formula for success – structuring your answer

Writing about short written texts is a little different to writing about extended texts (such as novels) or visual text (such as film), because you must write about two texts within your one answer. As a result, you should aim to write approximately 5 or 6 paragraphs in response to short written text questions.

It is important that you structure your answer carefully and clearly.

Step 1: Think about *The Question*
Look closely at the question. Look at the key words and decide how many parts the question has.

Example question	Question analysis
Describe a symbol or an object in each text. Explain, with detailed reasons, why each symbol/object was important.	This question has two parts: • Describe a symbol or an object. • Explain why the symbol/object was important. You must answer both parts of the question for text 1 and then again for text 2.

Step 2: Think about The Ideas
Aim to write approximately six paragraphs – brainstorm what the focus of each paragraph will be and make specific notes related to your text.
(In the following table, *Paragraphs 1 and 4* relate to the first part of the *Example question*, *Paragraphs 2, 3, 5 and 6* relate to the second part of the *Example question*, as outlined in the *Question analysis* above.)

Read, study and understand a number of short written texts **39**

Focus of paragraph	Example brainstorm using the short story texts, *On the Sidewalk Bleeding* and *The Last Spin*, by Evan Hunter
Paragraph 1 Describe a symbol or an object from text 1	The jacket – purple with 'The Royals' boldly printed across back; name over heart
Paragraph 2 Explain the 1st reason why the symbol/object from text 1 is important	It is why Andy is stabbed and why no one helps him
Paragraph 3 Explain the 2nd reason why the symbol/object from text 1 is important	It becomes the focus of his last minutes alive, as he struggles to remove it
Paragraph 4 Describe a symbol or an object from text 2	The gun
Paragraph 5 Explain the 1st reason why the symbol/object from text 2 is important	It is why the boys meet – game of Russian roulette
Paragraph 6 Explain the 2nd reason why the symbol/object from text 2 is important	It stops their friendship from developing – Dave is killed

Step 3: Think about *The Structure* of your Answer

Write your answer using the PDR structure.

The PDR paragraph structure

A paragraph should be focused, coherent, and well developed. Paragraphs are unified around a main point, and all sentences in the paragraph should clearly relate to that point in some way. The paragraph's main idea should be supported with specific information that develops or discusses the main idea in greater detail.

Each new paragraph should begin with a clear point **(P)**. This point should then be followed by appropriate development **(D)** and specific reference to the text **(R)**.

P = **P**oint is made – a single sentence which sets up the focus of the paragraph.

D = **D**evelop the point – explain clearly what you mean in 2 or 3 sentences.

R = **R**efer to a specific moment/ event/ conversation/ quotation from the text.

You should try and write 5 or 6 paragraphs in response to the question.

Using the PDR structure

Example question:

'Describe a symbol or an object in each text. Explain, with detailed reasons, why each symbol/object was important.'

Example answer:

Evan Hunter focuses both his stories, 'On the Sidewalk Bleeding' and 'The Last Spin', on an important object. In the short story 'On the Sidewalk Bleeding' he uses **the important symbol of the Royals Jacket.** *The jacket is the main character's prized possession. It is bright purple silk and has 'The Royals' boldly printed across the back. On the front his name, 'Andy', is smoothly written in black thread over his heart.* Andy is proud of being a Royal, **"*He was a Royal. There had been meaning to the title.*"**

The jacket is important because it is the reason Andy is lying bleeding on the sidewalk and that no one helps him. *He is stabbed by a rival gang called the Guardians*

P = **Bold**

D = *italics*

R = ***bold and italic***

and he hears a voice saying "That's for you, Royal!" *It is because the Guardians hate the Royals and because he was wearing the purple jacket that he is attacked. The jacket also prevents people from coming to his aid.* **When a young couple Freddie and Angela come across Andy by accident in the alley they are afraid to help him.** *They also only see the jacket and they don't want to get involved in the gangs' rivalry. Freddie says to Angela, "I don't want to get mixed up in this. He's a Royal."*

The jacket is also important because Andy spends the last moments of his life trying to remove it. *He realises as he lies there dying that the jacket stereotypes him. As Andy struggles to take off his 'Royals' jacket he visually signals to the reader the importance of retaining a sense of your own individuality.* **He struggles out of the jacket with pain ripping through his body.** *Being part of a group had once seemed very important to him but as he lies dying he realises that being Andy, the individual, is more important.* **We're told that he realises, "The jacket was a stupid meaningless thing that was robbing him of his life."** *Sadly the jacket continues to stereotype him even after his death.* **The policeman's response, "A Royal, huh?" shows the idea that this is simply one of many gang killings.** *It is as if real people aren't involved, only innumerable faceless members of meaningless gangs. Andy didn't die – only a Royal.*

In the short story 'The Last Spin', Evan Hunter **uses the object of the gun.** *The gun is a Smith and Wesson .38 Police Special. It has a sawn-off two-inch barrel and the handle is checked walnut. It is finished in a flat blue. The gun lies in the centre of the table along with three cartridges.*

The gun is important because it is why Tigo and Dave, the two main characters, are together in the basement room. *They belong to two rival gangs. Dave's club went into Tigo's gang's territory the night before. To settle the dispute both Dave and Tigo have been picked to represent their club in a match of Russian roulette. The gun brings them together and as they each take turns at spinning the cylinder and putting the gun to their head, they talk. Through their conversation they realise how much they have in common. Both of them are interested in joining the Army, they both have girlfriends and neither of them particularly likes the people in their gang.*

The gun is also important because it stops the likely development of their friendship. *Eventually they build up the number of cartridges in the cylinder to three, meaning there is a 2:1 chance of it firing. They decide to stop after one 'last spin'. They arrange to meet at the lake on Sunday and take their girlfriends out on a boat together. Sadly this doesn't happen.* **Dave fires the 'last spin' and an explosion rocks the basement room, ripping away half of his head. Tigo puts his head on the table and cries.**

Task 1
Using a PDR template

Using two of the texts you have studied in class, answer the same question as modelled above. Follow the structure and guidance given by the template.

Question:

'Describe a symbol or an object in each text. Explain, with detailed reasons, why each symbol/object was important.'

> The answer template is set out in the following manner:
> - **PDR** is indicated by **P**oint, **D**evelop and **R**efer.
> - The beginning of each paragraph has been started for you; this is in **bold**.
> - The text in *italics* is guidance on how to continue, what to add, etc.

Read, study and understand a number of short written texts **41**

Both the texts, *(title)* _____ **, by** *(author)* _____ ,
and *(title)* _____ **, by** *(author)* _____ , **have an important symbol/object.**
In the story *(title of text 1)* _____ **the** _____
is an important *(object/symbol – select the appropriate word)* _____ .
(Develop the first sentence with a full detailed description of the object or symbol**)**

_____

_____

_____

_____

_____

_____

_____

(Point**) This is an important object/symbol** *(delete one)* **because** _____
_____ .
(Develop further what you mean and **R**efer to specific moments/details from the text**)**

_____

_____

_____

_____

_____

_____

(Point**) It is also an important object/symbol** *(delete one)* **because** _____
_____ .
(Develop further what you mean and **R**efer to specific moments/details from the text**)**

_____

_____

_____

_____

_____

_____

_____

(**P**oint) **In the story** *(title of text 2)* _____ **the** _____
is an important *(object/symbol – select the appropriate word)* _____ .
*(**D**evelop the first sentence with a full detailed description of the object or symbol)*

_____
_____
_____
_____
_____
_____
_____

(**P**oint) **This is an important object/symbol** *(delete one)* **because** _____
_____ .
*(**D**evelop further what you mean and **R**efer to specific moments/details from the text)*

_____
_____
_____
_____
_____
_____

(**P**oint) **It is also an important object/symbol** *(delete one)* **because** _____
_____ .
*(**D**evelop further what you mean and **R**efer to specific moments/details from the text)*

_____
_____
_____
_____
_____
_____
_____

Task 2
NCEA Level 1 Practice Question
'Explain with detailed reasons how each text made you feel. Explain why each made you feel this way.'

> A model answer for short story is provided in the answer section for *A Game of Cards* and *Tangi*, by Witi Ihimaera.

Step 1: Think about the question
This question has two parts:
- Explain how each text made you feel.
- Explain why each text made you feel this way.

You must answer both parts of the question for text 1 and then again for text 2.

Step 2: Think about the ideas
Brainstorm the focus of your 6 (or 5) paragraphs:

General focus of paragraph	Specific focus using your text
Paragraph 1	
Paragraph 2	
Paragraph 3	
Paragraph 4	
Paragraph 5	
Paragraph 6	

Step 3: Using the PDR structure, write your own answer

Task 3

NCEA Level 1 Practice Question

'Choose at least three uses of language you enjoyed in each text. Explain why you enjoyed them.'

> A model answer for poetry is provided in the answer section for *Daffodils*, by W Wordsworth and *The Road not Taken*, by R Frost.

Step 1: Think about the question

This question has two parts:
- Choose three uses of language you enjoyed.
- Explain why you enjoyed them.

You must answer both parts of the question for text 1 and then again for text 2.

Step 2: Think about the ideas

Brainstorm the focus of your 6 (or 5) paragraphs:

General focus of paragraph	Specific focus using your text
Paragraph 1	
Paragraph 2	
Paragraph 3	
Paragraph 4	
Paragraph 5	
Paragraph 6	

Step 3: Using the PDR structure, write your own answer

Continue on your own paper if necessary.

Task 4

NCEA Level 1 Practice Question
'Think up a new title for each text. Explain why each would be a good new title.'

> A model answer for short story is provided in the answer section for *The Fat Boy*, by Owen Marshall and *Dear Mr Cairney*, by Graeme Lay.

Step 1: Think about the question
This question has two parts:
- Provide a new title for each text.
- Explain why each would be a good title.

You must answer both parts of the question for text 1 and then again for text 2.

Step 2: Think about the ideas
Brainstorm the focus of your 6 (or 5) paragraphs:

General focus of paragraph	Specific focus using your text
Paragraph 1	
Paragraph 2	
Paragraph 3	
Paragraph 4	
Paragraph 5	
Paragraph 6	

Step 3: Using the PDR structure, write your own answer

Continue on your own paper if necessary.

Task 5
NCEA Level 1 Practice Question
'Explain clearly what you think the author's purpose was in each text.'

> A model answer for poetry is provided in the answer section for the poems, *The Show* and *Exposure*, both by Wilfred Owen.

Step 1: Think about the question

This question has one part only:
- Author's purpose for writing each text (ie author's reason/ideas, etc).

You must answer the question for text 1 and then again for text 2.

Step 2: Think about the ideas

Brainstorm the focus of your 6 (or 5) paragraphs:

General focus of paragraph	Specific focus using your text
Paragraph 1	
Paragraph 2	
Paragraph 3	
Paragraph 4	
Paragraph 5	
Paragraph 6	

Step 3: Using the PDR structure, write your own answer

48 English Achievement Standard 1.4

Continue on your own paper if necessary.

NCEA Level 1 Questions

In the exam you will be provided with five pages of ruled lines for writing your answer in the Achievement Standard 1.4 question.

You should practise all of the topics below – however, you only have to write on one in the exam. Use your own paper to answer each question.

1. Describe an **idea** that **interested** you in **each** text.
   Explain **why** these **ideas interested** you.

2. Describe an **important place or period (time)** in **each** text.
   Explain **why** they were **important**.

3. Describe several language techniques used in **each** text.
   Explain **why** they were **important**.

4. Describe an **important incident** in **each** text.
   Explain **why** each incident was **important**.

5. Describe a **character** in **each** text.
   Explain **what** was **interesting** about **each** character.

6. Describe **at least ONE technique of structure*** used in **each** text.
   Explain **why** each technique was **important**.

   * This could include the use of links, sequence, layout, and any other interesting techniques the writer has used.

Read, study and understand a visual or oral text

NCEA Achievement Standard 1.5
Externally assessed
2 credits

Visual and oral texts include Film, Drama production, TV programme, Radio programme and Electronic text.

You will be required to write approximately 200 words in response to one of the questions offered in the external Achievement Standard examination – it may be necessary to write more than this to achieve 'Merit' or 'Excellence'.

You should spend approximately 25 minutes on answering the question.
- Answer all parts of the question.
- Use clear, well-chosen points.
- Back up your points with relevant reference to the moments/events from the text.

Show that you have thought about and reacted to the characters, events and issues in the text.

Assessment criteria

Show you have studied/know the text well

Show that you have thought about, and reacted to, the characters, events and issues in the text

Convey original insights

Achieved	Merit	Excellence
• Show **understanding** of one oral or visual text, using **evidence**.	• Show understanding of and **respond to** oral or visual text using **supporting evidence**.	• Show **perceptive** understanding of and response to one oral or visual text, using supporting evidence.

Reference to moments/events from the text (this could include quotation)

Well-chosen, relevant reference to moments/events from the text (this could include quotation)

Types of questions

Question category	Examples
Character	• How a character changes, grows • Character relationships • An important character • What a character learns • The challenges a character faces • Character conflict

Theme	• The main idea(s) of the text (message or issue) • Key moments that raise an important theme • What you are encouraged to think about
Plot	• The relevance of the beginning • An important moment/event • The climax • The effectiveness of the conclusion
Setting	• Time • Place • Social environment • The impact on characters, events, etc
Style/ Production techniques	• The effective use of language • Literary devices, such as figurative language • Narrative voice • Film techniques, such as, camera work, music/sound, lighting, special effects, props, costume, graphics, dialogue

Formula for success – structuring your answer

Step 1: Think about *The Question*
Look closely at the question. Look at the key words and decide how many parts the question has.

Example question	Question analysis
Describe a character that faces challenges in the text and explain how he or she faced the challenges.	This question has two parts: • Describe the character and the challenges she/he faces. • Explain how she/he faced the challenges.

Step 2: Think about *The Ideas*
Aim to write 4 or 5 paragraphs – brainstorm what the focus of each paragraph will be and make specific notes related to your text.

(In the following table, *Paragraph 1* relates to the first part of the *Example question*, *Paragraphs 2–4* relate to the second part of the *Example question*, as outlined in the *Question analysis* above.)

Focus of paragraph	Example brainstorm using the text *What's Eating Gilbert Grape?* directed by Lasse Hallstroom
Paragraph 1 Describe the character and the challenges she/he faces	Gilbert – 'father figure', has lots of responsibilities, finds his autistic brother and obese mother a burden, feels trapped
Paragraph 2 Explain the 1st way she/he faced the challenges	By making jokes about his mother's weight; eg calls her "a whale"
Paragraph 3 Explain the 2nd way she/he faced the challenges	By trying to keep Arnie (his brother with autism) in his sight and under control all the time
Paragraph 4 Explain a 3rd way she/he faced the challenges	Loses control – screams at Ellen about Arnie's birthday party and hits Arnie when he won't cooperate and get in the bath

Step 3: Think about *The Structure of your Answer*

Write your answer using the PDR structure.

The PDR paragraph structure

A paragraph should be focused, coherent, and well developed. Paragraphs are unified around a main point, and all sentences in the paragraph should clearly relate to that point in some way. The paragraph's main idea should be supported with specific information that develops or discusses the main idea in greater detail.

Each new paragraph should begin with a clear point **(P)**. This point should then be followed by appropriate development **(D)** and specific reference to the text **(R)**.

P = **P**oint is made – a single sentence which sets up the focus of the paragraph.

D = **D**evelop the point – explain clearly what you mean in 2 or 3 sentences.

R = **R**efer to a specific moment/ event/ conversation/ quotation from the text.

Remember, you should try and write 4 or 5 paragraphs in response to the question.

Using the PDR structure

Example question:

'Describe a character that faces challenges in the text and explain how he or she faced the challenges.'

The character Gilbert Grape in the film 'What's Eating Gilbert Grape?' directed by Lasse Hallstrom faces a number of challenges. The main challenge for Gilbert is that he is trapped, hence the title 'What's Eating Gilbert Grape?' *Gilbert is trapped by his obligations to his family. He is a caring person and devotes much of his time to his autistic brother, Arnie. Arnie needs lots of love, time and attention to ensure he is properly cared for, especially since their mother, Bonnie, is obese and unable to do much to look after her children. Although Gilbert loves his brother and mother, he feels that there is no escape from looking after them.* ***Gilbert often says to Arnie, "We're not going anywhere," and his opinion of living in Endora is "nothing ever happens, and nothing ever will."***

One way in which Gilbert faces his challenges is by making jokes about his mother's weight. *Even though Gilbert loves his mother, he also feels frustrated by her inability to carry out a parental role in the home, because of her physical condition. He manages his frustration and feelings of being burdened by using humour to relieve his anxiety.* ***This is shown when we see Gilbert hold some young children up to the window of his house so the boys can look at his mother and he refers to her as "a whale" when talking with his friends.***

Another way in which Gilbert faces his challenges is by trying to keep his brother Arnie in his sight and under control all the time. *Gilbert works at a grocery store and often he takes Arnie to work with him so that he knows where he is and what he is up to. Arnie also goes with Gilbert when he makes deliveries during the day. By having Arnie as a 'constant companion' he is able to care for him and try to keep him out of trouble.* ***We can see the trouble Arnie gets into when Gilbert is not there to supervise him, for example, he climbs a very high water tower without realising the risks and stays in a cold bath all night.***

At some points in the film Gilbert is unable to face and deal with his challenges and he loses control, becoming verbally and physically abusive. *Gilbert faces a large number of challenges and feels increasingly trapped by them and there are times where he is less able to deal with the obligations imposed on him.* ***The audience is aware of this when he screams at Ellen when she accuses him of doing nothing to organise Arnie's 18th birthday party and when Gilbert hits Arnie when he is being uncooperative and won't get in the bath.***

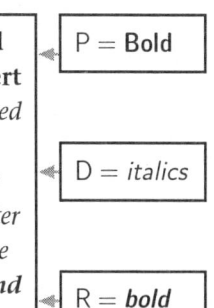

P = **Bold**

D = *italics*

R = ***bold and italic***

52 English Achievement Standard 1.5

Task 1
Using a PDR template

Using the text you have studied in class, answer the same question as modelled above. Follow the structure and guidance given by the template.

Question:

'Describe a character that faces challenges in the text and explain how he or she faced the challenges.'

> The answer template is set out in the following manner:
> - **PDR** is indicated by **P**oint, **D**evelop and **R**efer.
> - The beginning of each paragraph has been started for you; this is in **bold**.
> - The text in *italics* is guidance on how to continue, what to add, etc.

In the text, *(title)* _____ **, by** *(director)* _____ ,

a character who faces challenges is *(name a main character)* _____ .

This character is *(briefly describe the character)* _____

_____ .

The challenges he/she faces are *(briefly describe the challenges he/she faces)* _____

_____

_____

_____

_____

_____

_____

(Point**) One way in which the character faces the challenges is by** _____

_____ .

(Develop *further what you mean and* **R**efer *to specific moments / details from the text)*

_____

_____

_____

_____

_____

_____

(Point**) Another way in which the character faces the challenges is by** _____

*(**D**evelop further what you mean and **R**efer to specific moments / details from the text)*

(**P**oint) **Finally, the character also faces the challenges by** ....

....

*(**D**evelop further what you mean and **R**efer to specific moments / details from the text)*

Answering Plot Questions

The plot means what happens in a story, and why it happens. A TV documentary may have no plot. In film, radio or a stage play, the plot is important, especially the development of *conflict* and the *climax*.

It is not adequate to just rewrite the plot of the text in your answer to the question. You will not gain 'Achieved' if you only write a plot summary. You must show an understanding of the other features of an oral or visual text, so that you can link events to the features.

The main events typically start with a brief 'set up' period where important characters are introduced, details of the setting are established, etc. The story then gets underway with the introduction of the 'catalyst', an event that starts the tension mounting. The events then build to a climax, the point of highest tension in the story. This is typically followed by a short 'wind down' period, called the resolution or denouement.

Task 2
The plot of your text
Complete the graph following, by selecting and recording the main events of your text on the blank lines provided.

Climax – the point of highest tension

The beginning – the setting is established, characters introduced, etc

The catalyst – the event that starts the story's focus/main action

Task 3

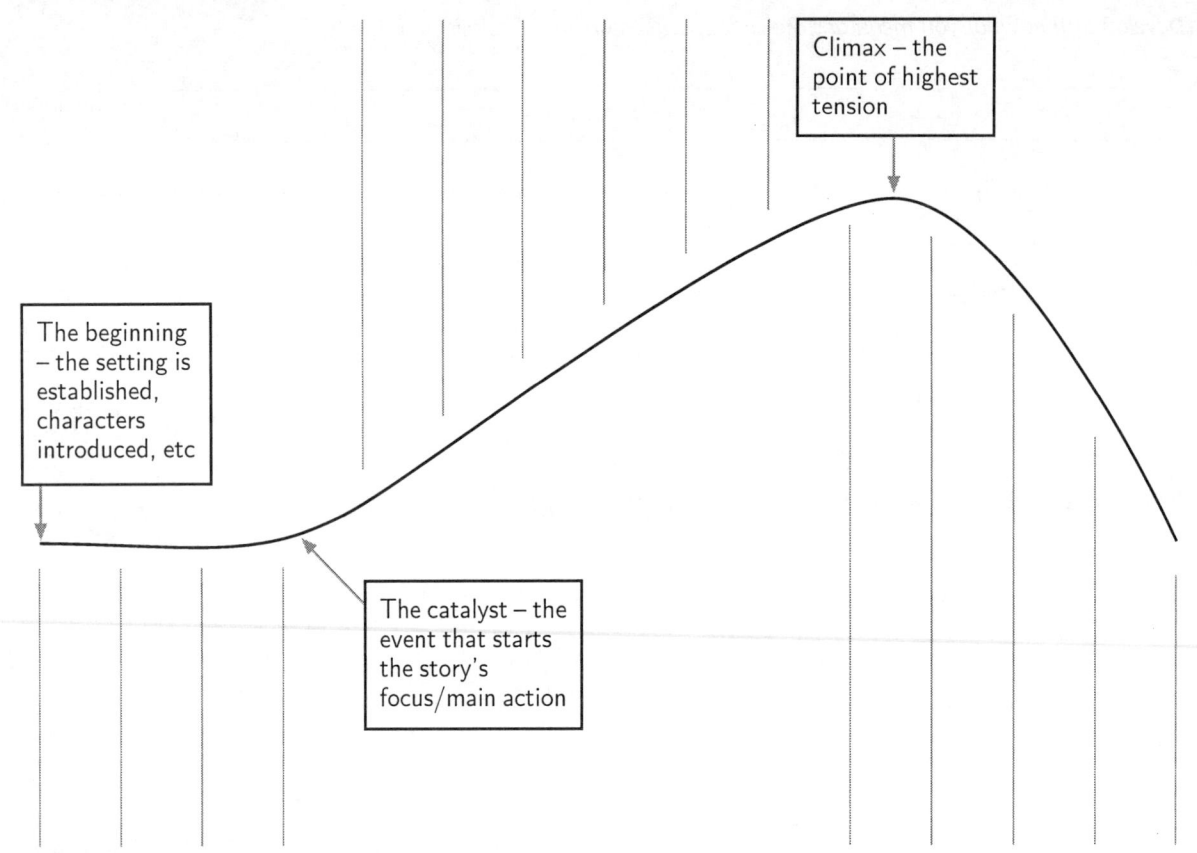

Practice Question for the plot

'Describe an important scene or event in your text and explain why it was important.'

A model answer is provided in the answer section for *Grace* by Pat Spillane.

Step 1: Think about the question

This question has two parts:
- Describe an important scene or event.
- Explain why it was important.

Step 2: Think about the ideas

Brainstorm the focus of your 4 (or 5) paragraphs.

General focus of paragraph	Specific focus using your text
Paragraph 1	
Paragraph 2	
Paragraph 3	
Paragraph 4	

Step 3: Using the PDR structure, write your own answer

_____

Continue on your own paper if necessary.

Task 4
Practice Question for the plot
'Describe the beginning and/or ending of your text. Explain why you would describe it as effective.'

A model answer is provided in the answer section for *What's Eating Gilbert Grape?* by Lasse Hallstroom.

Step 1: Think about the question
This question has two parts:
- Describe the beginning and/or ending of the text.
- Explain why you would describe it as effective.

Step 2: Think about the ideas
Brainstorm the focus of your 4 (or 5) paragraphs.

General focus of paragraph	Specific focus using your text
Paragraph 1	
Paragraph 2	

56 *English Achievement Standard 1.5*

Paragraph 3	
Paragraph 4	

Step 3: Using the PDR structure, write your own answer

_____
_____
_____
_____
_____
_____
_____
_____
_____
_____
_____
_____
_____
_____
_____
_____
_____
_____

Continue on your own paper if necessary.

Answering Character Questions

A **character** is a person (or sometimes an animal, ghost, etc) that appears in a text.

If you are writing about a non-fiction programme, remember that the characters have not been created by the author but are real people. You can still write about their personality and what the programme shows us about them.

Texts generally have major characters and minor characters.
- Major characters are those that are central to the events and ideas of the story.
- Minor characters, whilst not the focus of the story, may contribute on a lesser scale to events and ideas.

Character questions can also explore character relationships, character change/growth, character action and reaction.

Read study and understand a visual or oral text **57**

Task 5
The characters of your text
Consider the oral or visual text you studied in class and fill in the boxes below. You may have to take up less or more room than is given.

Main characters in my text are:	Minor characters in my text are:

Important relationships in my text are:	Characters who grow or change in my text are:

Task 6
Practice Question for character
'Describe an important person in your text and explain what made him or her important.'

> A model answer is provided in the answer section for *Kevin's Sentence* produced by Bob Carty.

Step 1: Think about the question
This question has two parts:
- Describe an important person.
- Explain what made him or her important.

Step 2: Think about the ideas
Brainstorm the focus of your 4 (or 5) paragraphs.

General focus of paragraph	Specific focus using your text
Paragraph 1	
Paragraph 2	
Paragraph 3	

58 English Achievement Standard 1.5

Paragraph 4	

Step 3: Using the PDR structure, write your own answer

_____

_____

_____

_____

_____

_____

_____

_____

_____

_____

_____

_____

_____

_____

_____

_____

_____

_____

Continue on your own paper if necessary.

Task 7

Practice Question for character

'Describe the most important relationship in your text. Explain how this relationship influences events.'

> A model answer is provided in the answer section *What's Eating Gilbert Grape?* directed by Lasse Hallstroom.

Step 1: Think about the question

This question has two parts:
- Describe the most important relationship in the text.
- Explain how it influences events.

Step 2: Think about the ideas

Brainstorm the focus of your 4 (or 5) paragraphs.

Read study and understand a visual or oral text **59**

General focus of paragraph	Specific focus using your text
Paragraph 1	
Paragraph 2	
Paragraph 3	
Paragraph 4	

Step 3: Using the PDR structure, write your own answer

_____
_____
_____
_____
_____
_____
_____
_____
_____
_____
_____
_____
_____
_____
_____
_____
_____
_____ *Continue on your own paper if necessary.*

Answering Setting Questions

The **setting** is where events happen (place) and when they happen (time). It also includes the social conditions of the era/place. For example, if the film is set in a private boys' college, then the social conditions would include the wealth and expectations of the school and families.

Questions typically focus on how the setting influences the events or affects the characters, etc. Depending on the text, the setting can be important or unimportant.

Task 8
The setting of your text
Consider the book you studied in class and complete the table below. You may need less or more room than is given.

Place setting	Country	
	City/town	
	Important places where action happens (eg a school, a farm, etc)	
Time setting	Era/year	
Social setting	Things happening around that time	

Task 9
Practice Question for setting
'Describe the setting of the text and explain how the setting is shown to be important.'

> A model answer is provided in the answer section for *Romeo and Juliet* directed by Baz Luhrmann.

Step 1: Think about the question
This question has two parts:
- Describe the setting.
- Explain how it is shown to be important.

Step 2: Think about the ideas
Brainstorm the focus of your 4 (or 5) paragraphs:

General focus of paragraph	Specific focus using your text
Paragraph 1	
Paragraph 2	
Paragraph 3	
Paragraph 4	

Step 3: Using the PDR structure, write your own answer

_____
_____
_____
_____
_____
_____
_____
_____
_____
_____
_____
_____
_____
_____
_____

Continue on your own paper if necessary.

Answering Theme Questions

The **theme** is the central idea of the text – the message(s) or issue(s) you are invited to think about while you are reading the text.

Themes generally emerge from the characters' actions and reactions. What they do, say and think about help us, the reader, focus on some important ideas that the author also wants us to think about.

Task 10

The theme of your text

Consider the book you studied in class and complete the table below. You may need less or more room than is given.

Important ideas the reader is encouraged to think about in the text	Events/characters that encourage us to think about the idea
1.	
2.	
3.	

Task 11

Practice Question for theme

'Explain an important idea in the text and explain how this idea is shown to be important.'

> A model answer is provided in the answer section for *Billy Elliot* directed by Stephen Daldry.

Step 1: Think about the question
This question has two parts:
- Explain an important idea.
- Explain how the idea is shown to be important.

Step 2: Think about the ideas
Brainstorm the focus of your 4 (or 5) paragraphs:

General focus of paragraph	Specific focus using your text
Paragraph 1	
Paragraph 2	
Paragraph 3	
Paragraph 4	

Step 3: Using the PDR structure, write your own answer

Continue on your own paper if necessary.

Answering Production Technique Questions

The techniques used to produce oral and visual texts are important and affect the way we appreciate them. When you write about production techniques, you must connect the technique with the other features of the text – eg, how the camera work shows a particular character.

Your answer needs to explain how the technical features – camera work, soundtrack/music, lighting, costume, dialogue, special effects, props, etc – work to make the text more effective.

You may be asked to write about two or three different production techniques used in your text.

Task 12
Production techniques used

Consider the text you studied in class and complete the table below. You may need less or more room than is given.

Production techniques used	How the techniques make the text more interesting/powerful/effective
1.	
2.	
3.	

Task 13
Practice Question for Production Techniques

'Describe at least TWO production techniques that work well in the text and show how they are important. You could choose from the following: music, dialogue, lighting, graphics, colour, props, special effects, costume, soundtrack, camera work, etc.'

> A model answer is provided in the answer section for _White Squall_ by Ridley Scott.

Step 1: Think about the question

This question has two parts:
- Describe a production technique that works well in the text.
- Show how the production technique is important.

Remember to write about TWO different production techniques.

Step 2: Think about the ideas

Brainstorm the focus of your 4 (or 5) paragraphs:

General focus of paragraph	Specific focus using your text
Paragraph 1	
Paragraph 2	
Paragraph 3	
Paragraph 4	

Step 3: Using the PDR structure, write your own answer

Continue on your own paper if necessary.

NCEA Level 1 Questions

> In the exam you will be provided with five pages of ruled lines for writing your answer for the Achievement Standard 1.5 question.
>
> You should practise all of the topics below – however, you only have to write on *one* in the exam.
>
> Use your own paper to answer each question.

1. Describe an **idea** that **interested** you in the text.
   Explain **why** this **idea interested** you.

2. Describe an **important place or period (time)** in the text.
   Explain **why** it was **important**.

3. Describe at least **TWO production techniques*** in the text.
   Explain **why** they were **important**.
   * This could include music, dialogue, lighting, graphics, colour, props, special effects, costume, soundtrack, camera work, layout, use of space, use of links, or any other important techniques used.

4. Describe an **important incident** in the text.
   Explain **why** it was **important**.

5. Describe a **character** in the text
   Explain **what** was **interesting** about the character.

6. Describe **one or more important structural techniques*** used in the text.
   Explain **why** it was/ they were **important**.

   * This could include the use of transitions, links, sequencing, layout, scene divisions, or any other important techniques used.

Read and show understanding of unfamiliar texts

NCEA Achievement Standard 1.6
Externally assessed
3 credits

Achievement Standard 1.6 assesses your ability to read and show understanding of unfamiliar texts.

The word 'text' for Achievement Standard 1.6 covers a variety of texts, such as:
- Written text – creative or formal, prose or poetry.
- Visual text – a static image, a storyboard from a film, a cartoon or image from a magazine.
- Oral text – the written transcript of a speech, or a script from a stage or radio play.

You should spend approximately 45 minutes on the external examination.

This chapter will focus on skills required and provide practice tasks for reading unfamiliar texts.

There will be questions which allow you to achieve at all three levels for each text. In general, the first question on each text will be at an 'Achieved' level, followed by the 'Merit' and 'Excellence' level questions. Some questions allow you to achieve 'Merit' or 'Excellence' depending on the level of your response.
- 'Achieved' – answer *any* 7 questions correctly.
- 'Merit' – must correctly answer a further 5 questions at 'Merit' or 'Excellence' level.
- 'Excellence' – must correctly answer a further 4 questions at 'Excellence' level.

Achievement criteria

Know what the text is about

Word choice, sentence structure, organisation of ideas

Achieved	Merit	Excellence
Show **understanding** of unfamiliar texts and **identify the ideas** and/or **style** and/or **language features**.	Show **understanding** of unfamiliar texts through **explanation** of ideas and/or style and/or **language features**.	Show **understanding** of unfamiliar texts through **explanation and appreciation** of ideas and/or style and/or language features.

| What is the main point/message of the text? | Pun, rhetorical question, repetition, etc | Provide some detail from the text to support your understanding | Shows a higher level of thinking, able to provide a personal, perceptive response |

Strategies for Success – Answering the Questions

Step 1: Key words and parts of the question

Read the question and underline the **key words**. Key words might be the specific language feature you are asked to identify, or directions you need to follow. For example, 'What is the meaning…', 'In your own words…', 'imperative', 'euphemism', etc.

Identify whether the question has one or more parts. Note this on the exam paper.

Step 2: Read the unfamiliar text
Read carefully, looking for the answers to the questions as you go. Write on the text or highlight pieces you will want to come back to when writing your answer. You may need to read each piece of text more than once.

Step 3: Write your answers
Be careful to follow the instructions and answer all parts of the question. Try to express your answers clearly. Attempt to answer *all* the questions. To achieve 'Merit' and 'Excellence', answers will require more detail and depth of discussion. If necessary, use more paper to continue your answers.

Step 4: Re-read the question and answer
Re-read the question and your answer.
- Have you done what was asked of you?
- Is your answer easy to understand?
- Have you written enough for the Merit/Excellence questions?

Task 1
Good knowledge of language techniques is very important. Fill in the grid at the bottom of the page, by matching the right example with the right technique.

Example	Technique
1. The tree scratched at the window.	a. Pun
2. I doubt anyone here wants that to happen?!	b. Personification
3. Drink + Drive = Grave Result	c. Onomatopoeia
4. The opposition whipped our debating team.	d. Hyperbole
5. Run, run before you're seen!	e. Euphemism
6. The better team won on the day.	f. Repetition
7. There were millions of people at the show.	g. Cliché
8. An analogue multi-meter which provides 62 measuring ranges.	h. Jargon
9. I'm between jobs at the moment.	i. Rhetorical question
10. He's a beaut old bloke.	j. Imperative
11. The dogs were howling.	k. Slang
12. Go to your room!	l. Colloquial language
13. She stared silently at the sky.	m. Alliteration
14. She was as skinny as a rake.	n. Metaphor
15. The sky was full of diamonds.	o. Simile

1.	2.	3.	4.	5.	6.	7.	8.	9.	10.	11.	12.	13.	14.	15.
b														

NCEA Level 1 Questions

Reading Written Texts

1. Celebrating Being Māori and Healthy **article**

> ### It's Infectious
>
> Mihi Austin loves being Māori and working in the health area. It infiltrates everything she says and does and her passion for it is simply infectious.
>
> Mihi works for one of the country's largest Māori health provider organisations based in Auckland. 'Our focus is on health promotion but we see ourselves as supporting Māori
> 5 development <u>across the board</u>. We are driven by what we believe are our rights – it's our right as Māori to have good oral health care, it's our right to have good hospital care, these are our rights as citizens of this land. That is what we promote and encourage.'
>
> Mihi staunchly believes that Māori health providers have made a big difference to Māori health. A good example is Rikki. 'I used to hang out with my mates rather than go to school.
> 10 I smoked heaps and ate junk food. By the time I was 17 I was in a real bad way – overweight, unfit. Thanks to Mihi my life changed and because of her I wanted to change my lifestyle – I went back to school, stopped smoking, ate properly and slowly got fit. I felt better about myself, stronger as a person and now I feel really proud of what I have achieved.
>
> I feel good about being Māori, and because of people like Mihi I'm now working with Māori
> 15 kids in a Māori way. I'm helping them feel good about being Māori too.'
>
> And that approach appears to have got people off their bums. 'We've helped to change behaviours and expose Māori to opportunities they may not have heard about or been interested in before. We've provided access and choice to whole communities of people,' says Mihi.
> 20 We've made Māori come together. We're celebrating being Māori, and getting healthy and fit messages across at the same time. Now that's a real health outcome for me – it's about measuring how good Māori feel about being Māori and we've definitely contributed to that.
>
> 'Change can only come from us. We know <u>information is power</u>. We work on the basis that if we inform a hundred people, they'll inform a hundred more and so on. Then we begin
> 25 to take back a bit of power over our lives and make changes we want as people of the land.'
>
> Adapted from 'Celebrating Being Māori and Healthy' pp. 36–37 *Mana*, No. 3 April–May 2001

a. Identify the pun in the first paragraph.

b. What is the meaning of the phrase 'across the board' in line 5?

c. According to the article, how has Mihi made a significant difference to Rikki's life?

d. In your own words, explain what Mihi means in the final paragraph when she says that 'information is power'.

_____

_____

_____

_____

2. *Boy Fishing* **poem**

Boy Fishing

He sits in a bright
morning of bush
and sea

the water is green
5   and deep
beneath him

the legs of the jetty
slide
<u>slish, slish, slish</u>
10   against the strange
sigh and salt
of the tide.

<u>The wind waits
behind an island</u>
15   the eye of his pipi
sways
beneath a wave

his summer of rock-pools
shellfish
20   and curious pieces
of glass is scattered
across the bay.

He holds his breath –
"something is taking
25   the bait," he says tightening
the line
taking the strain
standing
and raising his small rod
30   sharply.

*He's probably caught
a stone
a piece of driftwood
passing by
35   a canvas shoe
filled with sand*

a tangled shadow
of seaweed.

He sees launches
40   rocking
at the wharf
tourists stepping on board
for the Cream Trip

his father's friends
45   pulling dinghies
from safe harbours
of dry sand.

His back bends.

He holds the purr
50   of his plastic reel

the flash
of his varnished rod

the lively dance
of his nylon line
55   in the braided weight
of the sea.

He is a boy
in a bright green
morning

60   a man
in his shiny day.

Stephanie de Montalk, 'Boy Fishing', *Jewels in the Water* ed. Terry Locke, Leaders Press, The University of Waikato, 2000.

a. Identify the specific language feature used in 'the wind waits behind an island' in lines 13 and 14.

b. What is the boy using for bait?

c. In the *italicised* lines (31–38), someone else is watching the boy fishing. Explain in your own words what that person is thinking.

d. What is suggested by repeating the word 'slish' in line 9?

72 English Achievement Standard 1.6

Reading Visual Texts

1. Promotional film advertising New Zealand **storyboard**

a. What camera shot is used in Shot 10?

_____

b. What is the likely target audience for this promotional film? Support your answer with evidence from the text.

_____

_____

c. Explain the links between the words used in the opening and closing shots 'Wild New Zealand' and 'Adventure New Zealand' and the images in the storyboard.

_____

_____

_____

_____

© ESA Publications (NZ) Ltd, Freephone 0800-372 266

Read and show understanding of unfamiliar texts **73**

2. *Greenpeace* **advertisement**

Is the food that you buy at the supermarket GE Free?

Like it or not, you and your family could be eating genetically engineered (GE) food.

In New Zealand we don't have any commercial GE crops - yet. Greenpeace is campaigning for a GE free New Zealand, but we need your help to keep it that way.

Exercise your right to buy GE free foods by checking out our website: www.greenpeace.org.nz/truefood/ for a comprehensive list of GE free food producers.

Greenpeace needs your support to continue campaigning for a GE Free New Zealand. Call 0800 22 33 44 or mail your donation to Private Bag 92 507, Wellesley St, Auckland.

GREENPEACE

SAY NO TO GE.
The choice is in your hands

a. In the advertisement, what do the letters 'GE' stand for?

_____

b. Identify an imperative (command) used in the advertisement.

_____

74 English Achievement Standard 1.6

   c. Explain a link between the purpose of the advertisement and the bar code.

_____

_____

_____

Reading Oral Texts

1. Student speech extract

>   He mihi tuatahi ki te Atua. Ko ia
>   te tīmatatanga me te whakamutunga
>   o ngā mea katoa.
>
> 5   I begin my speech with
>   the greeting to your God who
>   is the beginning and end of
>   all things in your life.
>
>   Ka huri ōku whakaaro ki a rātou –
>   ngā tīpuna.
>
> 10 I now turn my thoughts
>   to your ancestors.
>
>   E ngā mate, haere haere haere.
>   Haere ki te wā kāinga.
>
>   May the people in your life
> 15 who have died go to a resting place.
>
>   Tātou te hunga ora kia tātou
>   Tena koutou, Tena koutou,
>   Tena koutou katoa.
>
>   To us the living
> 20 Greetings to ALL of you.
>
>   I greet you in the language of the Māori.
>   I greet you in the language of the Pākehā.
>   I greet you in the language of Aotearoa.
>
>   <u>Language is a lens</u>. It is how we see each other.
>
> 25 When I speak to you in your language, you not only understand me but you feel
>   recognised – you feel warm – mahana.
>
>   But it's even better if I pronounce your name correctly. If you are a Māori boy called
>   Hemi and the teacher calls you '<u>Hee-my</u>,' if you are a Pākehā girl called Sarah White and
>   the teacher calls you Sarah '<u>Fee-tay</u>' then the teacher is making no effort to show you
> 30 respect. That teacher needs glasses!
>
>   It's a feel-good factor in a bicultural country – but not only that – I say
>   Talofa, Sione
>   Bula, Shamira
>   Malo e lelei, Numia.
>
> 35 So how do you see things?

Read and show understanding of unfamiliar texts **75**

a. Identify the figure of speech or language device used in 'language is a lens' (line 24).

b. Why are the words 'Hee-my' (line 28) and 'Fee-tay' (line 29) written in speech marks?

c. In your own words, explain the main idea in the final five lines of the extract.

2. Student speech extract

> … It's a self-hate orgy which the fashion industry pushes onto us all the time. We're bombarded with images in the media constantly telling us that we all want to be, indeed need to be, stick-thin models if we are to be attractive to ourselves and others. Be a bag of bones!
>
> 5 Models, the beautiful people on screen and in print, are fat free. In New Zealand, we are told, 80% of women are within their 'normal' body weight but only 18% see themselves as normal. Therefore we subject ourselves to a constant series of primitive tortures designed to help us conform to the media image of beauty.
>
> Our view of our own body image determines our behaviour and how we describe
> 10 ourselves. 'My thighs are <u>soooo</u> fat!, you're so much prettier than I am', and so on.
>
> It's impossible to escape the body image message in magazines and on TV. Not a day goes by when we're not looking at ourselves as fat! Images of ideal beauty only come in one size, and that's fat free!
>
> Whether you are short, tall, skinny or fuller figured, I hope you can accept your body.
> 15 But I'm telling you to do more than that. You should jump off the bandwagon. It's so yesterday to be in the self-hate group when it comes to how you see your body.

a. Why is 'soooo' (line 10) written in this way?

b. In the final paragraph, find a euphemism for the word 'fat'.

c. In your own words, explain a main point put forward by the speaker about body image.

AME Workbooks for NCEA Level 1
MATHEMATICS
ENGLISH
SCIENCE
Workbook
Other AME titles for NCEA Level 1 also available

Deliver a speech in a formal situation

NCEA Achievement Standard 1.7
Internally assessed
3 credits

Achievement Standard 1.7 assesses your ability to prepare and present a speech in a formal situation. Generally, your classroom teacher will guide you as to the topic and purpose of your speech.

Assessment criteria

	Achieved	Merit	Excellence
Ideas	• Speaks in a formal situation to communicate ideas with **supporting detail**. *Give examples, such as your experiences, research, references*	• Speaks in a formal situation to communicate ideas with supporting detail and **explanation**. *Give reasons for your ideas*	• Speaks in a formal situation to communicate ideas **convincingly** with supporting detail and explanation. *You make your audience want to believe you*
Language	*There is an introduction, series of points and conclusion* • **Structures content** and uses language and a level of formality appropriate to the audience, situation and purpose.	*You use varied and interesting types of sentences* • Structures content and **uses language** and a level of formality **appropriate to the audience, situation and purpose**. *Suitable for the people and occasion*	• Structures content and uses language and a level of formality appropriate to the audience, situation and purpose, **with effect**. *Use language in such a way that your audience is affected*
Voice and body skills	*Everyone can hear* • Speaks **audibly** to an audience using some appropriate eye contact, **variation of voice** and body language. *Change volume, speed and stress to suit the point you are making*	• Speaks audibly to an audience with some confidence using appropriate eye contact, variation of voice and **body language**. *How you use movements to support your speech*	• Speaks audibly to an audience with confidence and impact, using voice, eye contact and body language for **deliberate effect**. *You use your skills in a controlled way*

Writing the speech

To write a successful speech, follow the 7 steps outlined below

Step 1: Decide on a topic
Using the guidelines given to you by your teacher, try to select a topic that you have some prior knowledge of so that you can focus on writing. Ensure your classroom teacher approves of your choice of topic.

Step 2: Brainstorm some ideas on the topic
Think about what role you are taking on as the speaker, what is the situation and what is your purpose in giving the speech? What information is needed in your speech to fulfil its purpose? What ideas might the listeners find interesting? What detail will you need to clearly explain your ideas?

Do you have enough material to speak for at least three minutes?

Step 3: Organise the ideas logically
Provide 'coathangers' for your listener to hang your ideas on in your introduction, the body of the speech and in the conclusion. The spoken word is gone immediately, and so listeners have nothing to refer to, so use 'coathangers' such as, firstly, secondly, thirdly.

Step 4: Use language features
This could include personal pronouns (you, us, I, etc), rhetorical questions, repetition.

Step 5: Write an interesting/catchy introduction
Following is an example of an effective introduction – the speaker gains the audience's attention.

> I have no respect. I wound without killing. I break hearts and ruin lives. I am cunning, spiteful and gather strength with age. The more I am quoted the more I am believed. I flourish at every level of society. My victims are helpless. To track me down is impossible. I have no name, no face. The harder you try to find me, the more elusive I become. I am nobody's friend. I tarnish reputations; they are never the same again. I can topple governments, wreck marriages and ruin careers. I cause sleepless nights and heartache. I spawn suspicion and generate grief. Even my name hisses with spite. I am Gossip.
>
> We've all been guilty of gossiping at some point in our lives and as this poem from *Chicken Soup For the Soul* highlights, gossip can be incredibly damaging.

The introduction is effective because:
- It personifies 'gossip', giving it human qualities.
- Creates interest/suspense – who is *I*?
- Uses a poem which may already be known by some in the audience.

Task 1

The Introduction
Write the introduction for your speech in the space provided below. Think about using techniques to make the introduction catchy and effective.

Introduction _____

_____

_____

_____

_____

_____

Step 6: Write the body of your speech

Include four or five different ideas, supported with convincing detail and explanation. Try to provide clear links between each idea so that the listener can easily follow your points.

Following is an extract from the body of a speech on 'Gossip'. The speaker has supported their ideas with detail and explanation and provides links (highlighted in *italics*) between the ideas (highlighted in **bold**).

> "So, why do people gossip? Once could say that it's just **human nature to gossip** about others. Men may claim that **gossip is purely a female occupation**. As humans we want to know about other people, **we are naturally curious**. Gossip can even be seen as a **leisure pastime**. Gossip is what makes life interesting. *Interesting for the gossiper, that is!*
>
> *Gossip is far from interesting* for those being gossiped about. Gossiping about others involves personally attacking their being …
>
> **Sensationalised magazine headlines** encourage us to indulge in the tragedy and despair of celebrities and heroes. **'Adam and Sally's New Love', 'Karen Olsen's Tragic Times!'** *This is nothing more than* **gossip thinly disguised as news**.
>
> *In a similar way* TV shows such as 'Holmes' revel in the murky side of New Zealand's elite."

Task 2
Body of the Speech

Outline the four/five ideas you will include in the body of your speech. Remember to provide detail and explanation to support your ideas.

Idea	Detail/explanation

Step 7: Write an effective conclusion

Your conclusion should draw your ideas together, link to the purpose of the speech and finish in a convincing manner.

Read the following conclusion from a speech on 'Gossip'. Look at how the speaker has linked the conclusion with the introduction (highlighted in *italics*), how they have drawn their ideas together (highlighted in **bold**) and managed to conclude in a convincing manner.

> Novelist, Zora Hurston described gossip as "Words walking without masters". Words with no control can have a devastating effect. Yet, gossip can't be blamed on a single individual, it takes more than one person to gossip. **What is needed is for all of us, at school, at work and in the media, to take more personal responsibility for what we say and how we say it.**
>
> Take the time to consider the impact of your words on the person you are talking about.
>
> *Consider the monster you have created – with gossip as its tongue!*

Task 3
The Conclusion

In the space below write an effective conclusion for your speech. Try to include some of the ideas modelled above.

Conclusion

_____
_____
_____
_____
_____
_____
_____
_____
_____
_____
_____
_____

Using the notes you have made for the **Introduction**, **Body** and **Conclusion** (in **Tasks 1**, **2** and **3**), you should now be able to write your whole speech. Do this on your own paper.

Delivery of your speech

Allow enough time to learn and rehearse your speech thoroughly so that you can give a confident presentation on the day of assessment. Consider how you can most effectively deliver your speech and practise it a number of times *before* the day.

It is useful to make **delivery notes** in the margins alongside your speech as you rehearse. Some delivery techniques may come about naturally when you look at the content and purpose of each piece. In particular, focus on:

- **Voice** – volume, pace, tone, pitch, pause – think about which words/phrases you wish to emphasise or where you may wish to give your audience time to think about an idea.

Deliver a speech in a formal situation **81**

- **Eye contact** – maintain eye contact with your audience, use longer gazes to emphasise particular points.
- **Gesture/facial expression** – where can you build in natural gesture to highlight a certain idea or word? Ensure your expression on your face relates to the tone of your speech (eg if the speech is serious, it would be inappropriate to be smiling).
- **Stance** – aim to stand in a steady, yet relaxed manner. Avoid excessive and/or nervous movements (such as swaying, moving from leg to leg), which may distract from the content of your speech.

Delivery techniques

In the following speech introduction, the words to be emphasised are **bolded**. The *italic directions* [in square brackets] indicate the voice and body techniques used by the speaker immediately after that point.

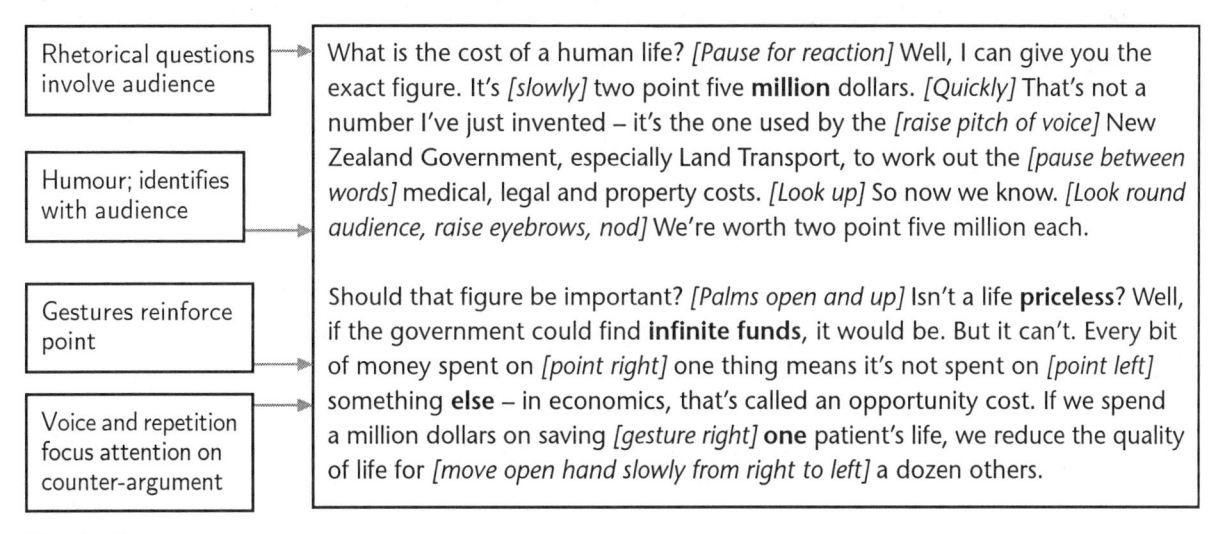

Rhetorical questions involve audience →	What is the cost of a human life? *[Pause for reaction]* Well, I can give you the exact figure. It's *[slowly]* two point five **million** dollars. *[Quickly]* That's not a number I've just invented – it's the one used by the *[raise pitch of voice]* New Zealand Government, especially Land Transport, to work out the *[pause between words]* medical, legal and property costs. *[Look up]* So now we know. *[Look round audience, raise eyebrows, nod]* We're worth two point five million each.
Humour; identifies with audience →	
Gestures reinforce point →	Should that figure be important? *[Palms open and up]* Isn't a life **priceless**? Well, if the government could find **infinite funds**, it would be. But it can't. Every bit of money spent on *[point right]* one thing means it's not spent on *[point left]* something **else** – in economics, that's called an opportunity cost. If we spend a million dollars on saving *[gesture right]* **one** patient's life, we reduce the quality of life for *[move open hand slowly from right to left]* a dozen others.
Voice and repetition focus attention on counter-argument →	

Task 4

Using the following introduction of a speech, write appropriate delivery notes and practise techniques of eye contact, voice and body language for each of the highlighted blocks of text. The first example has been done for you.

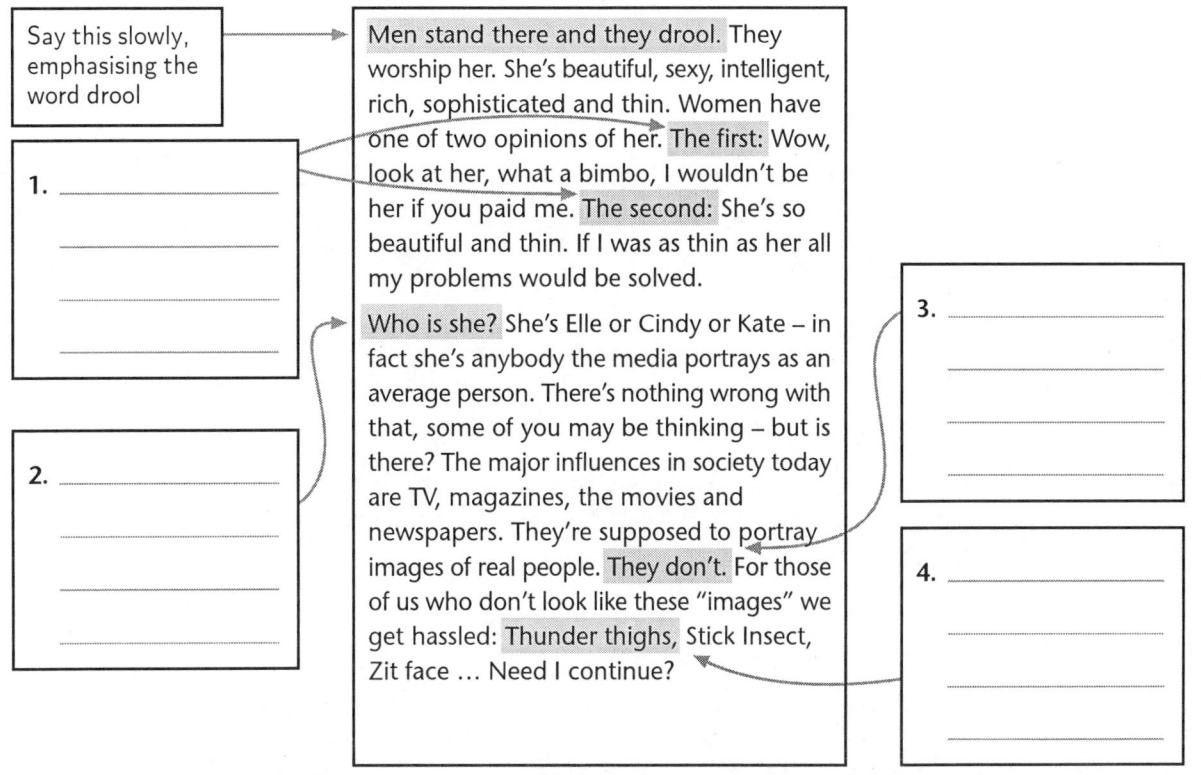

Say this slowly, emphasising the word drool	Men stand there and they drool. They worship her. She's beautiful, sexy, intelligent, rich, sophisticated and thin. Women have one of two opinions of her. The first: Wow, look at her, what a bimbo, I wouldn't be her if you paid me. The second: She's so beautiful and thin. If I was as thin as her all my problems would be solved.
1. _____	
2. _____	Who is she? She's Elle or Cindy or Kate – in fact she's anybody the media portrays as an average person. There's nothing wrong with that, some of you may be thinking – but is there? The major influences in society today are TV, magazines, the movies and newspapers. They're supposed to portray images of real people. They don't. For those of us who don't look like these "images" we get hassled: Thunder thighs, Stick Insect, Zit face … Need I continue?
	3. _____
	4. _____

© ESA Publications (NZ) Ltd, Freephone 0800-372 266

Using the annotations you have made and checked for **Task 4**, you should now be able to annotate your own speech. Do this on your own paper.

Final preparation for Assessment Day

Write your speech (or just key words) onto **cue cards**. You should know your speech well enough to only need to refer to the cue cards for the briefest of moments, if at all.

You may like to indicate some delivery techniques on the cue cards by using red pen or underlining to remind you of where to place emphasis. Some speakers write brief delivery notes on the cue cards (such as 'Pause', 'Say slowly', 'Frown') as reminders of the techniques they wish to use.

Try to be calm on the day. Everyone finds public speaking challenging – it's the number one fear in the world! Use deep breathing, have a drink of water before you start speaking, aim to begin confidently. Be well prepared and you will have every reason to be positive.

Produce a media or dramatic presentation

NCEA Achievement Standard 1.8
Internally assessed
3 credits

Achievement Standard 1.8 may involve the production of a media presentation or a dramatic presentation.

- **Media presentation** – a Poster, advertisement, storyboard or other static image; a Web page or website; a PowerPoint display; an Audio tape / radio show; a Short film; or a Newspaper (a front page). The media presentation must be demonstrated. You must present it so that your teacher can assess it. This will include being able to identify verbal and visual techniques used and their intended effect.
- **Dramatic presentation** – a Dramatic monologue; a Scene from a play; a Role play; or Performance poetry. A dramatic presentation must be performed. You have to get up in class and present it so that your teacher can assess it. This will include being able to identify verbal and visual techniques used and their intended effect.

Assessment criteria

	Achieved	Merit	Excellence
Ideas	Ideas are simple • Communicates **straightforward ideas** in a presentation for a **specific audience and purpose**. Suitable for the task and audience set by the teacher	Ideas are linked to others, more complex • Communicates **developed** ideas in a presentation for a **specific audience and purpose**.	Ideas draw the presentation together, perceptive • Communicates **fully developed** ideas in a presentation for a **specific audience and purpose**.
Techniques	• Uses appropriate **verbal and visual/dramatic** techniques. Gesture, facial expression, eye contact, stance	Voice; tone, volume, pitch, pace, variation • Uses appropriate **verbal and visual/dramatic** techniques **with effect.** Techniques used achieve the desired response, eg anger, sympathy	• Uses appropriate **verbal and visual/dramatic** techniques **with striking and/or original effect.** Techniques are used naturally; ideas are innovative, creative, insightful
Identifying techniques	• **Identify** verbal and visual/dramatic techniques used and **their intended effect.**	• **Identify** verbal and visual/dramatic techniques used and **their intended effect.**	• **Identify** verbal and visual/dramatic techniques used and **their intended effect.**

84 English Achievement Standard 1.8

> The first part of this Chapter will focus on **Static images** and the second part will focus on **Dramatic Monologue**. Breaking the chapter into these two parts provides planning and presentation strategies to apply to either of these types of tasks.
>
> Check with your teacher exactly what your Achievement Standard 1.8 task will require, as there are a number of options they could select.

Media presentation – Static Images

The following will help you produce a static image as a media presentation, as well as write a commentary identifying the techniques used and their intended effect. A model static image and commentary are provided (on pages 86/87).

> The example used throughout is based on communicating an idea from a short story; the short story used is *The Escalator* by Witi Ihimaera.

The presentation of your static image will involve *Planning* and *Drafting* stages.

Step 1: Planning

The static image needs to reflect a **main idea** from the text.

Fill in the following boxes for the static image you are presenting.

Text chosen:

The main idea/message is:

A relevant quote from the text is:

Verbal and visual techniques

You must decide what verbal and visual techniques you will use and what their intended effect is.

It is best to make these decisions *before* you do a draft of the static image, then you will have the relevant material needed for the commentary about the image.

Example

Technique	Detail – where used?	Intended effect
Dominant image	Escalator, as the teeth of a crocodile.	To show the fearsome effect the escalator had on Miriama.

Task 1

Planning a static image

Use the table following to help you plan your static image.

This is not a complete list of verbal/visual techniques – there may be others you should consider using.

Technique	Detail – where used?	Intended effect
Dominant image		
Layout		
Proportion		
Lettering		
Colour		
Symbols		
Verbal technique /quote selected from the text		

Step 2: Drafting

It is important to draft your image by thinking carefully about the reasons behind each choice you make.

Task 2

The Draft

Complete a draft of your static image (on your own paper).

Include the visual and verbal techniques you have used in your planning. Consider the use of white space on your static image; you do not want your image to be too cluttered or have too much white space around the image.

Ask yourself and others (eg parents/friends/teacher) 'Is the main idea communicated clearly and are the verbal and visual techniques used with effect?'

Step 3: Writing the commentary

Below is a commentary discussing the verbal and visual techniques used in the static image based on *The Escalator* by Witi Ihimaera.

The commentary is annotated in the following way:
- Useful words used to explain the intended effect of techniques are **in bold**.
- Intended effect is shown <u>by underlining</u>.
- Techniques used are in *italics*.

"She looked up that frightening silver tunnel. She looked down and saw the black divisions between each step, appearing from beneath the silver footplate."

> **Commentary**
>
> On my static image I have used a range of symbols, and a quotation from the text to **convey** the main ideas from the short story 'The Escalator' by Witi Ihimaera.
>
> *The dominant image is the escalator.* I have used a crocodile to give the effect of the escalator moving upward, into its' jaws. This **shows** the fearsome effect the escalator has on Miriama.
>
> *The quotation I have chosen to place on my image* is used to **signify** Miriama's thoughts about the escalator. "She looked up that frightening silver tunnel. She looked down and saw the black divisions between each step appearing from beneath the silver footplate". The font I have used is 'curlz' to **show** that nothing in life is simple, there is always a twist, whether it's an obstacle or a fear to overcome.
>
> The 'black divisions' are a part of the escalator, but they also **represent** the division between the worlds.
>
> *I have used the colours black and red in my image.* These are to **indicate** feelings and emotions. I have used red on the jagged image around Hiriama's face to **show** anger and embarrassment. The black on the escalator symbolises fear of the unknown.
>
> *Other images/symbols I have used include the world with a split down the centre to **show** the differences between the rural and urbanised worlds.* The sun **represents** Gisborne, Miriama's home town and the tick shows this is what is familiar or 'right' to Miriama. The Beehive building **represents** Wellington and the question mark **suggests** that it is an unknown, confusing city for Miriama.

Task 3

The Commentary

Write your own commentary about your static image using the following template. Refer back to the planning table for the visual/verbal techniques used and their intended effect.

Avoid making comments such as 'I used red as it makes it stand out' or 'I put a large roulette wheel on the image to catch people's attention'. Comments such as these do *not* discuss the 'intended effect' of the techniques in adequate detail.

The text that I have based my static image on is _____

and the main idea in the text that I have conveyed is _____

The dominant image I have chosen to use on my static image is _____

This represents _____

I have selected the quotation _____

to emphasise/show _____

Continue using the structure outlined in the template above to write the rest of your commentary. Use paragraph starters related to the various visual/verbal techniques used.

_____
_____
_____
_____
_____
_____
_____
_____
_____
_____
_____

Dramatic Presentation – Presenting a Dramatic Monologue

The following will help you to plan, write and perform a dramatic presentation as outlined to you by your classroom teacher. You may be asked to write a monologue including key ideas about a character from a text you have studied, or you may have to write interview questions and answers related to the challenges a character faces in a text you have studied.

Think about what TV and film actors do to make their characters realistic. What verbal and dramatic techniques can you use to make your character believable? You may also like to use costume and/or props. Although costume/props are not necessary to gain 'Achieved', their use may enable you to 'get into the role' more easily.

> The Example used throughout is based on the character Spider from the novel *Spider* by William Taylor.

Step 1: Planning

It is sensible to base your monologue on a reasonably major character, one who faces a number of challenges and who changes/develops throughout the text.

Character is: Spider from the novel *Spider* by William Taylor.

Important events/challenges in the script include:
- Deciding whether to enter the Goldman Piano Competition.
- Trying to form a relationship with Moana McKenzie.
- Finding out his mother is a stripper.
- Meeting his father for the first time.
- Preparing for the final of the Goldman Piano Competition.

Task 1

The character

My character is:

Important events /challenges included in the script:

1.
2.
3.
4.
5.

Step 2: Writing the Script

Assessment requires written interview questions and their answers.

The questions need to be open and reasonably direct, so that you can write answers which allow you to develop the character well for the audience.

- "Did you feel scared when…" – can only be answered with a yes/no, which would show limited knowledge/understanding of the character.
- "How did you feel when…" – offers the possibility to develop an answer, which would enable exploration of the character's reactions and feelings.
- You could include relevant quotations from the text within your script to build on the sense of 'real voice' of the character.

Question: Why did you decide to enter the Goldman Piano Competition?

Answer: I had to take some time to make this decision. That's why I took the entry form and went up to the pine trees where I do all my important thinking. I had never entered anything like this before. Bea, my music teacher, had never taken me down the 'traditional' path that other music students go down – not for me the recitals, exams – so this was a big step. I guess, looking back, that it was the next logical stage if music was to be my future – if I had any future. I had to decide whether I was entering the competition for Bea, or for my mum who has supported my music all these years, or because I really wanted to – for myself – and really that was the only valid reason for entering – to prove something to myself.

Task 2

Writing the Script

Using the character you have chosen in **Task 1**, write a question and answer in the spaces provided, using the model as your guide. (Write other questions and answers on your own paper.)

Try to have 5 or 6 questions and answers that demonstrate your knowledge of the whole text and that provide good development of character.

Question: _____

_____

Answer: _____

_____

_____

_____

_____

_____

_____

_____

Step 3: Verbal and Visual/Dramatic Techniques and Annotating the Script

Once you have written your script you need to consider the verbal and visual/dramatic techniques you will use to bring your character to life for the audience.

One way to do this is to read through the script aloud and note down the techniques you seem to use naturally. Then think about other techniques that may be effective given the content and situation:

- **Verbal techniques** – use of voice; think about your use of volume, tone, pitch, pace, pause, stress, etc.
- **Visual/dramatic techniques** – gesture; stance/movement; facial expression; eye contact.

Make notes on your script – what techniques will you use and what is the intended effect. You *must* do this to gain 'Achieved'.

An example of a part-annotated script follows.

(This part-annotated script also provides the basis for **Task 3**.)

Produce a media or dramatic presentation 91

Technique – stress/emphasis
Intended effect – to highlight the importance of

Question: Why did you decide to enter the Goldman Piano Competition?

Answer: I *had* to take some time to make this decision. That's why I took the entry form and went up to the pine trees where I do all my important thinking. I had never entered anything like this before. Bea, my music teacher, had never taken me down the 'traditional' path that other music students go down – not for me the recitals, exams – so this was a big step. I guess, looking back, that it was the next logical stage if music was to be my future – if I had any future. I had to decide whether I was entering the competition for Bea, or for my mum who has supported my music all these years, or because I really wanted to – for myself – and really that was the only valid reason for entering – to prove something to myself.

1. Technique _____
_____
_____
Intended effect _____
_____
_____

2. Technique _____
_____
_____
Intended effect _____
_____
_____

3. Technique _____
_____
_____
_____
Intended effect _____
_____
_____

4. Technique _____
_____
_____
Intended effect _____
_____
_____

5. Technique _____
_____
_____
Intended effect _____
_____
_____

6. Technique _____
_____
_____
Intended effect _____
_____
_____

Technique – gesture (indicate for my left for Bea, and to my right for Mum)

Intended effect – to show that Spider had people to consider other than himself

Task 3
Verbal and Visual/Dramatic Techniques and Annotating the Script
Add suitable verbal and visual features that would be effective for the other highlighted features not yet annotated in the script above.

Task 4
Annotating your own Script
Using the model above, carry out the annotation of your own script.

Step 4: Rehearsing the Presentation
Ensure you have completed the script and the annotation of techniques and intended effects in enough time to learn the script thoroughly before the assessment day. To really 'get into' the role of the character, you cannot be too reliant on notes. (Reliance on notes should be avoided, if at all possible.)

Try the following:
- Rehearse with a friend or family member.
- Rehearse in front of a full-length mirror – this helps you with eye contact.
- Tape the best delivery of your script that you can give – play it back regularly and follow along with the tape.

Try to use the visual and verbal techniques as naturally as possible in your performance. You want the performance to effectively portray your character, but you don't want to look like you are taking an aerobics class!

Assessment day

Try to be calm on the day. Everyone finds public performance challenging. Take time before you begin to breathe deeply and to 'become' the character you are about to be. This is where costume/props may be useful. Start in a convincing manner and work to sustain confidence throughout the performance.

By being well prepared, you can face the assessment day confidently.

Research, organise and present information

NCEA Achievement Standard 1.9
Internally assessed
3 credits

Achievement Standard 1.9 assesses your ability to carry out a research task and then organise and present the information and findings as a final product.

Achievement Standard 1.9 focuses on five main skill areas; your ability to:
- Plan a research topic.
- Gather useful information.
- Record the research process.
- Organise and present your findings.
- Draw conclusions and make judgements.

Your teacher will give you a specific research task and will provide you with clear instructions. The task given will vary from school to school; however, the skills assessed remain the same across all schools and all topics.

Assessment criteria

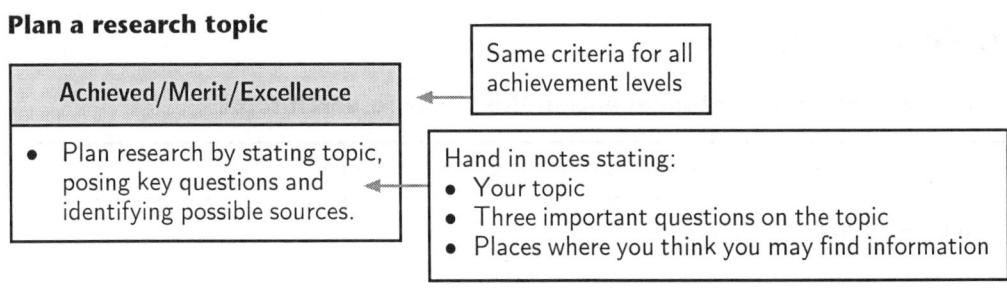

Plan a research topic

Achieved/Merit/Excellence — *Same criteria for all achievement levels*

- Plan research by stating topic, posing key questions and identifying possible sources.

Hand in notes stating:
- Your topic
- Three important questions on the topic
- Places where you think you may find information

Gather useful information

Achieved/Merit/Excellence — *Same criteria for all achievement levels*

- Collect, **select** and record relevant information, **recording** sources in an **accepted** format.

Choose what is useful

List every source you use, stating:
- Source
- Author/ creator
- Publisher/ owner
- Date of publication
- Usefulness of source

Follow your teacher's instructions/ guidelines

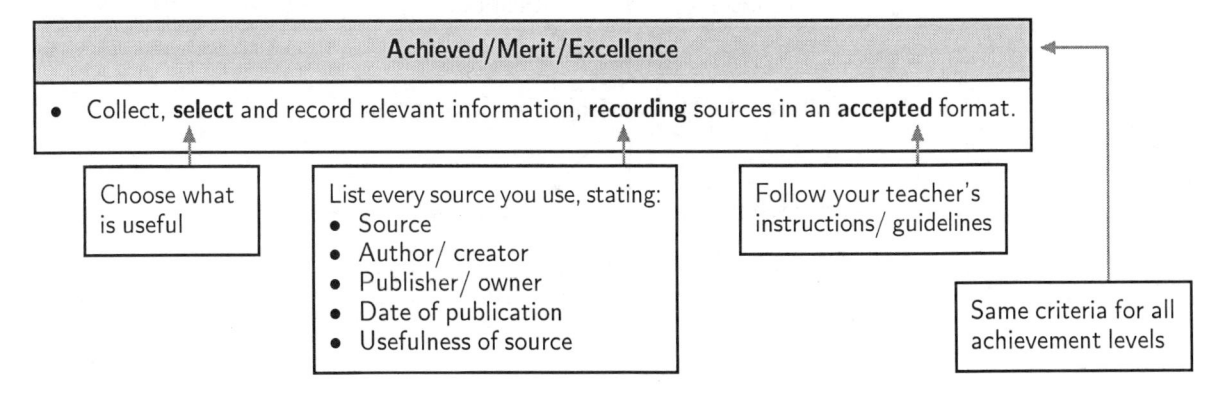

Record the research process

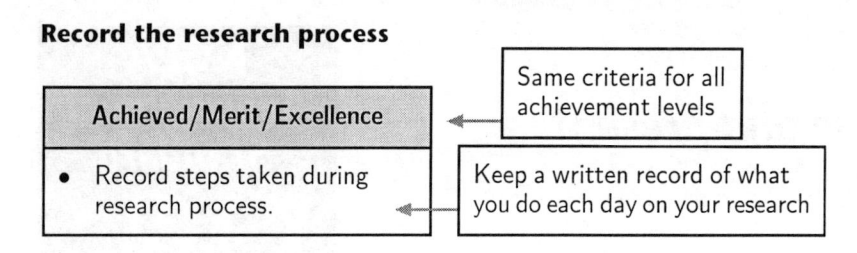

Achieved/Merit/Excellence	← Same criteria for all achievement levels
• Record steps taken during research process.	← Keep a written record of what you do each day on your research

Organise and present information – drawing conclusions and making judgements

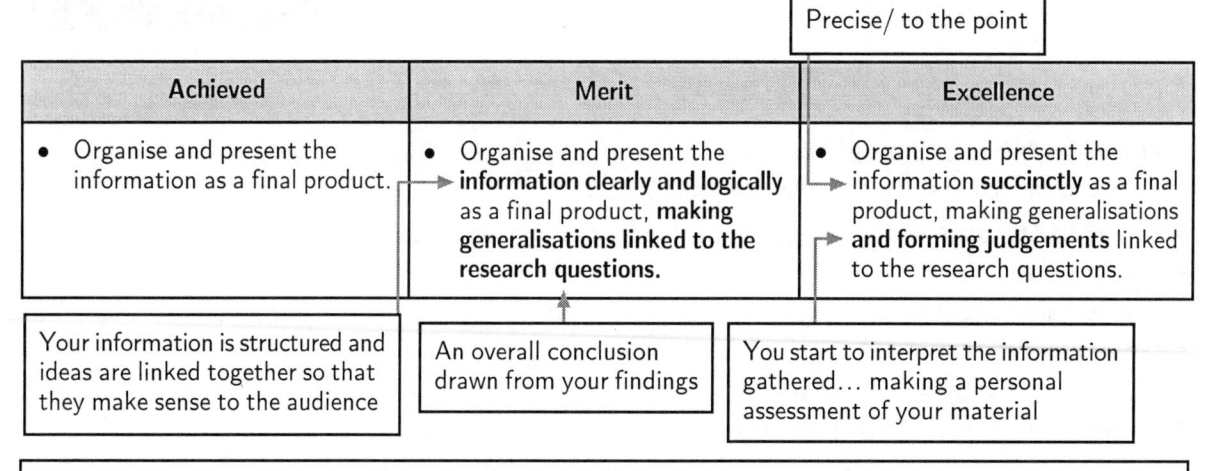

Achieved	Merit	Excellence
• Organise and present the information as a final product.	• Organise and present the **information clearly and logically** as a final product, **making generalisations linked to the research questions.**	• Organise and present the **information succinctly** as a final product, making generalisations **and forming judgements** linked to the research questions.

Precise/ to the point (→ Excellence)

Your information is structured and ideas are linked together so that they make sense to the audience (→ Achieved)

An overall conclusion drawn from your findings (→ Merit)

You start to interpret the information gathered… making a personal assessment of your material (→ Excellence)

Differences in achievement level are found only in your presentation of ideas.

The marker will be looking to see if your points are clear and logically ordered, if you make generalisations, and if you make judgements.

Planning a Research Topic

Step 1: Decide on your specific area of focus within the larger research topic

The example used throughout is based on the general topic 'New Zealand'.

An initial brainstorm could include the following:

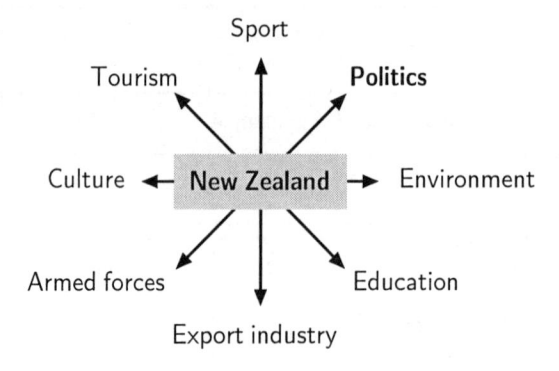

New Zealand →
- Sport
- Tourism
- Politics
- Culture
- Environment
- Armed forces
- Education
- Export industry

Task 1

Complete a similar brainstorm for the actual topic given to you by your teacher for Achievement Standard 1.9.

Step 2: Brainstorm your chosen area of focus

List everything that you know about the topic

For the general topic 'New Zealand', the specific area of focus within the larger research topic is 'Politics in New Zealand'.

Politics in New Zealand
• Jenny Shipley = 1st woman to become Prime Minister.
• Parties have 'seats'.
• Parties = Labour, National, Greens, ACT, NZ First, Alliance, United New Zealand.
• Centred at Beehive in Wellington.
• Helen Clarke = present Prime Minister.
• System = MMP.
• Democracy.

List things that you don't know about the topic

Use 'what you know' as a way of identifying things you don't know but could find out about.

For the general topic 'New Zealand', the specific area of focus within the larger research topic is 'Politics in New Zealand'.

What I know	What I don't know
• Parties have 'seats'.	• How many seats? What is the present division of seats? How is seat number allocation worked out?
• Two main parties = Labour and National.	• What are the philosophies of the various parties? How are they similar? How do they differ?
• Centred at the Beehive in Wellington.	• History of the Beehive? When was it built? Who by? Why is it called a 'beehive'?
• Jenny Shipley = 1st woman to become Prime Minister.	• When/how she became Prime Minister? What is the history of women in NZ politics?

Task 2

This Task is based upon the general topic 'New Zealand'; the specific area of focus within the larger research topic is 'Politics in New Zealand'.

List some questions that you could find out for each of the following areas.

1. Helen Clarke = present Prime Minister.	
2. System = MMP.	
3. Democracy.	
4. Other ideas:	

Task 3

Complete a brainstorm for the research topic you are investigating for Achievement Standard 1.9.

What I know	What I don't know

Step 3: Create key questions

Key questions focus your research on exactly what it is that you are trying to find out.

A good key question should be 'open'. 'Open' means the question is wide enough to allow you to find a range of information within the scope of the question.

Avoid 'closed' key questions (questions where the answer is limited, eg to a 'Yes', 'No', finite number, date, etc).

Task 4

This Task is based upon 'Politics in New Zealand'.

Consider the various questions listed below. Decide whether they are *open* or *closed* by ticking the appropriate box.

	Open	Closed
1. How many seats are there in parliament?	☐	☐
2. In what year did parliament first sit?	☐	☐
3. How did New Zealand's democratic system of government evolve?	☐	☐
4. How many parties are involved in parliament?	☐	☐
5. How do the philosophies of the two major parties differ?	☐	☐
6. Who was the first woman Prime Minister to be voted in?	☐	☐
7. How long does one government spend in parliament before the next election?	☐	☐
8. What does an MP's job involve?	☐	☐
9. How does the MMP system work?	☐	☐

Task 5

Use your brainstorm of 'What you know' and 'What you don't know' to help you create areas of interest/key questions for the research topic you are investigating for Achievement Standard 1.9 (identified in **Task 1**).

Key Question 1: _____

_____

Key Question 2: _____

_____

Key Question 3: _____

_____

Step 4: Brainstorm where information for the key questions can be found

Do not spend time looking for information in places not likely to assist your specific research. (For example, Encarta, an American encyclopaedia, is not likely to assist in a New Zealand-focused study.)

Aim to collect a range of source material (information on your topic). Try to include written, visual and oral sources.

Task 6

1. Below is a list of research technologies (methods of finding information) and sources (the information itself).

   Decide which are 'research technologies' and which are 'sources' by ticking the appropriate box.

	Research technology	Source
1. CD-ROM	☐	☐
2. Magazine articles, eg *Time* magazine	☐	☐
3. Photographs	☐	☐
4. Index New Zealand (online)	☐	☐
5. Television	☐	☐
6. TV programmes (eg *Holmes*, *60 minutes*, documentaries)	☐	☐
7. Letter	☐	☐
8. Knowledgeable person/specialist in the given field	☐	☐
9. Internet	☐	☐
10. Non-fiction book	☐	☐

2. List all the other research technologies and sources you can think of.

Task 7

Complete a list of sources which could be useful for the research topic you are investigating for Achievement Standard 1.9.

Gathering Useful Information

Step 1: Create and use key words
Key words help to find information. Think about how you can narrow your search by combining key words to focus specifically on what you are looking for.

Internet searches
Use speech marks (" ... ") to search for source material that has the same words in the exact order as you have typed them in to the search engine. Use the addition sign (+) to search for source material that includes both the words/phrases you have specified, but in no particular order.

Task 8
This Task is based upon 'Politics in New Zealand'.

Suggest three key words you could use if you were investigating the Key Question 'How did democracy come about in New Zealand?'

Key word 1: _____

Key word 2: _____

Key word 3: _____

Task 9
List relevant key words for the research topic you are investigating for Achievement Standard 1.9.

_____

_____

_____

Step 2: Be critical of information found
When collecting information, be critical of:
- *Who wrote the source information.* Anyone can post information on the internet. Try to ensure the author of any information (especially when using source material found on the internet) is suitably qualified in the given field of knowledge.
- *When the information was written.* Look closely at the date of publication of the material. Some non-fiction texts may have been published many years ago and the information may be dated in comparison with new discoveries or events.

Task 10
Explain *why/why not* it would be worth using the following source:

An essay titled, *The History of Democracy in New Zealand* by Chloe Brown, Victoria University, Year 1 student.

☐ Would use ☐ Would not use

Reason: _____

_____

Step 3: Select what part(s) of the source are useful to the research
Avoid photocopying or printing whole pages of information. Select only information that helps you answer your key questions. Scan the information and note-take or cut-and-paste the information that is relevant to your research.

For each source you use, formally record:
- Source.
- Creator.
- Publisher/owner.
- Date of publication.
- The useful information provided by the source, organised under each relevant key question.

Record the Research Process

Your teacher will tell you how she/he wants this done; typically you will be asked to keep a research log. The following Example is based upon the general topic 'New Zealand'; the specific area of focus within the larger research topic is 'Politics in New Zealand'.

Date	What I did	What I found
05/05	Used the key words *politics* and *Zealand* on the school library on-line catalogue.	Three books were listed: • *Politics, the basics* by S D Tansey. • *The New Politics: a third way for New Zealand.* • *From Welfare State to Civil Society* by Dr D G Green. *From Welfare State to Civil Society* had some very good information on the establishment of New Zealand's Welfare State.

Be as specific as you can in both these sections

Organising and presenting information – drawing conclusions and making judgements

- For 'Achieved' – must **present information** relevant to your key questions.
- For 'Merit' – must present relevant information and **then draw conclusions based on this information**.
- For 'Excellence' – must present relevant information, draw conclusions from the information and **then add personal judgements based on the conclusions you have made**.

> Think about a courtroom. The Judge hears a range of **information** relevant to the case. From this information they draw **conclusions** – eg, 'The person is guilty'. They then make their **judgement/ruling** – eg, "This is a serious crime and you are sentenced to ten years without parole!"

Look at the *conclusion* and *judgement* for the following three pieces of information:

Information

| A person got up at 7.30 am. | ⇒ | The person had no breakfast. | ⇒ | The person got a speeding ticket. |

Drawing a conclusion – the person got up too late!

Adding a judgement – the person needs better time management skills.

Task 11

Draw a *conclusion* and add your *judgement* based upon the following three pieces of information.

Information

| It was cold. | ⇨ | The beach was deserted. | ⇨ | The waves were crashing against the shore. |

Conclusion: _____

Judgement: _____

_____

Task 12

This Task is based upon the general topic 'New Zealand'; the specific area of focus within the larger research topic is 'Politics in New Zealand'. The following three extracts each answer a different key question and are taken from three different research reports.

Tick which category you think each extract falls into, bearing in mind:
- 'Achieved' is: Information only.
- 'Merit' is: Conclusion made.
- 'Excellence' is: Judgement made.

Extract 1

Key question: 'How do the philosophies of the two major parties differ?'

National is right of centre. For example they advocate tax cuts and user-pays systems. This means they believe that the individual can, and wants to, look after themselves. They don't believe in State control and believe the State should stay out of people's lives as much as possible. Labour is more left wing. Social spending tends to increase under a Labour government. Their policies are driven by the idea of society working collectively and believe that when people can't look after themselves the government should look after them.

☐ Achieved   ☐ Merit   ☐ Excellence

Extract 2

Key question: 'How is it that New Zealand adopted democracy?'

The majority of early settlers who came to New Zealand were from Great Britain and they brought the Westminster system of government with them – which is a democratic system of government.

☐ Achieved   ☐ Merit   ☐ Excellence

Extract 3

Key question: 'What does an MP's job involve?'

An MP is responsible to a wide range of people. They must represent the views of their electorate within the House of Representatives. They also have electorate offices where members of the public can speak with them directly, for example to seek assistance with a problem that the MP may be able to help with. MPs spend time on community activities such as speaking at public gatherings and visiting local schools. Their job is diverse and complex as it also involves the collection of in-depth information so that they can debate legislation knowledgeably. A lot of their work happens behind the scenes, they do far more than we realise and they have to have good people skills and communication skills to perform well.

☐ Achieved   ☐ Merit   ☐ Excellence

Answers

The 'Achieved', A, 'Merit' M, and 'Excellence' E, ratings given with the answers to NCEA questions for the externally assessed Achievement Standards chapters are based upon the professional judgements of the authors.

Achievement Standard 1.1

Tasks 1–3
Answers will vary.

Task 4
1. smooth, brown – adjectives; like warm pools of hot chocolate – simile.
2. Metaphor.
3. Onomatopoeia and/or alliteration.
4. Simile.
5. Adjectives.

Tasks 5 and 6
Answers will vary.

Task 7

Errors	Corrections
unreconisable (line 1)	unrecognisable
smoothness' (line 7)	smoothness (without the possessive apostrophe)
wouldnt (line 10)	wouldn't
radience (line 10)	radiance
comitting (line 12)	committing
She looked so sure of herself able and agile	She looked so sure of herself, able and agile (comma inserted)

Task 8
Answers will vary.

104 Answers

Achievement Standard 1.2

Task 1

Possible ideas include:
- Alcohol.
- Party drugs.
- Chat rooms / texting generation.
- Raves / dance parties.
- Fast cars.
- Relationships.
- Media influences.

Task 2

Possible ideas include:
- Younger people seem to be increasingly involved in adult types of behaviour.
- Temptations exist, but not all youths give in to the temptations.
- Modern youth don't have any more temptations than the previous generation – simply different temptations.

Task 3

Answers will vary.

Task 4

- Informal language use creates the wrong tone – the passage in general needs more formal vocabulary.
- Some of the sentences are far too long and uncontrolled.
- Abbreviations need to be removed, such as 'GM'.

An example of appropriate style for this introduction follows.

Genetic engineering is leading the way in the advancement of technology. Over the past 20 years, computers, cellphones and other information technology, such as the internet, have dominated the limelight of technology development. However, scientists in the 21st century are now focusing on new discoveries in the field of genetic engineering. Through genetic modification, more food could be produced, endangered species protected and extinct species recreated, cures for currently-incurable diseases found, or designer babies created. Whilst there are potentially great benefits to be gained from genetic engineering, many people in society consider the risks outweigh the benefits.

Task 5

Answers will vary.

Task 6

Errors	Corrections
benifits	benefits
scientists'	scientists
dinosors	dinosaurs
unatural	unnatural
babys	baby's
… curing 'incurable diseases' creating designer babies or recreating extinct animal species …	… curing 'incurable diseases', creating designer babies or recreating extinct animal species … (comma added)

Task 7

Answers will vary.

Achievement Standard 1.3

Tasks 1 and 2

Answers will vary.

Task 3

An important event in the novel 'Water in the Blood' by Alan Bunn is when Liam opposes Dave's authority by demanding to be let out of Dave's car on the way to the Daytona Raceway, after Dave causes an accident. This is important because it splits the friendship between Dave and Liam and leads to conflict. Up until this point Liam had accepted Dave's irresponsible behaviour.

One way that this event is important is that it is Liam's first step to individuality. Before this, Liam was content to follow Dave's lead, such as when he pulled a motorcyclist off her bike because Dave demanded it. However, at this point in the novel Liam takes a responsible stance by walking home and declaring he wasn't going to live with "one foot in the grave".

Another reason is that further conflict arose from this event. Dave hated Liam for undermining his perceived authority and tried to beat him up at school because Dave believed Liam had reported him to the police. This fight led to Dave's expulsion and Liam's suspension. During his time away from school, Liam had time to think about his future and committed himself to his schoolwork. "Somehow Liam had cracked the cast he had been set in and Dave didn't like it."

A third reason why this event is so important is that it allowed Liam to take up canoeing, a sport that Dave hated. Liam was looking for ways to develop new friendships and move away from Dave and Blair. Because Liam took up canoeing he developed better friendships with Anne and Craig and matured more. "The difference, he thought, was how Craig treated other people."

The final reason why this event is important is that this event and the resulting conflicts lead to the conclusion of the novel, with Dave realising he doesn't have a positive future and chooses to commit suicide by ramming a roadblock. "My spots are stuck fast." This reveals to the reader how Liam's life may have taken a different direction if he had not turned his back on Dave at the start. Liam still feels guilty about Dave's death, but as Craig tells him, "you didn't choose his life for him, he did." (**E**)

Task 4

Answers will vary.

Task 5

The most important relationship in the text 'Spider' by William Taylor is the one between Spider and his beloved piano. Spider shares a special bond with the piano, which was recognised by Bea McKenzie, Spider's piano teacher. Spider devotes a great deal of his time to practising his chosen art form and never complains about it, which displays his commitment.

Spider sacrifices a lot of the usual habits teenagers indulge in, for example 'having a social life'. Spider hardly ever goes out, and has very few close friends. But this doesn't seem to bother him. Spider sacrifices playing rugby in order to focus entirely on the piano. Although rugby meant a lot to Spider, he realises that without making sacrifices he wouldn't have been able to achieve such a close bond with his piano, and this is how one of the main themes, that of sacrifice, is revealed. Spider says, "I am doing what I have to do. As I say, to do what I want to do, I've got to run those miles."

Spider shares such a close relationship with his piano his mates consider him a bit 'woosy', particularly Bryson Brown. Spider gets given a hard time by Bryson because Bryson thinks he should be following something manly, like rugby. Bryson then makes it his duty to teach Spider how to be a 'real man', and consequently takes him out to town on his birthday to all the popular strip clubs. While they are at one particular club, Spider discovers, to his absolute horror, that his mother is the star attraction. Had Bryson not felt the need to make Spider more 'manly' and banish his piano-playing habits, Spider would have never found out about his mother's secret.

Because Spider is so devoted to practising the piano, he tends to isolate himself from the real world and the people around him. His school principal, Miss Simmonds, also allows him the time off school to continue to practise, particularly before his final performance in the Helene Goldman Piano Competition. He practices so much that his tutor, Bea McKenzie, has to force Spider to have a break and get out for a while. Spider doesn't seem to notice how isolated he's become because he is so devoted and committed to playing his piano.

Spider's relationship with his piano is an extremely influential part in him winning the Helene Goldman Piano Competition. While the other top three finalists were all very talented piano players, they did not share the same passion that Spider had while he was performing. The incredible amount of time Spider had spent practising the piece of Beethoven he performed was clearly evident in his performance. Because he knew the piece off by heart, bar by bar, note for note, he could give a much more passionate performance. All he wanted to do was share with the audience a favourite piece of music, composed by his idol, Ludwig van Beethoven. (*E*)

Task 6

Answers will vary.

Task 7

In the novel 'Goodnight Mister Tom' by Michelle Magorian, the setting plays an important role. The novel is set against the backdrop of World War II. In particular, it is set in England during 1939 and 1940. Most of the action takes place in a village called 'Little Weirwold'. Little Weirwold is a country village. It has a close-knit community, where everyone knows everyone. It is a very happy, friendly, bright and welcoming village. A second important location within the setting is that of London. London is the total opposite of Little Weirwold. London is war-torn and Willie, the main character, sees it as a cold, dark and violent place.

The setting is important in that is gives a sense of credibility to the story. People know about World War II, therefore they are able to believe the story when it talks about bomb raids and the children being evacuated into the country to be safe. The main character, Willie, is one of these children who are evacuated. It is because of the war that Willie is removed from his mother and experiences, for the first time in his life, a warm and loving environment.

Willie's experiences in the country village of 'Little Weirwold' allow him to grow and develop as a person. When he was living with his mother in London she abused him physically, mentally and emotionally. He lived in fear and often wet the bed as a result. His mother even sends a leather belt with Willie when he is evacuated so that the family he stays with also can discipline him. As a result of the abuse, Willie is withdrawn, alone and scared when he arrives at Mr Tom's house. The warmth and friendly atmosphere of Little Weirwold help Willie to become more confident and to enjoy life. He makes friends and eventually stops wetting the bed. He feels loved and secure.

It is also because of the setting that Mr Tom is forced to take someone into his home. Mr Tom had previously lost both his wife and his son, and he has isolated himself as a result. Mr Tom had forgotten how to love and he carried a lot of pain around inside himself. Had it not been for the war, Mr Tom may never have changed either. He has no choice in taking in an evacuee and it is through letting Willie into his house that he eventually lets him into his heart and learns to love and laugh again.

Lastly, the setting of the war also leads to Willie losing his dear friend, Zach. Will meets Zach in Little Weirwold, where Zach has also been sent as an evacuee. Zach's energy and love of life are infectious and help Will to come out of his shell. Together they have lots of adventures. Sadly, when Zach returns to London to be with his mother and father he is killed as a result of the bombing. Mr Tom is worried that Willie will withdraw into himself again. The story finishes with Will taking Zach's bicycle and careering off down the road – showing that Zach's impact on his life will not fade and that Willie will be all right. (*E*)

Task 8

Answers will vary.

Task 9

An important theme in the novel 'Looking for Alibrandi' by Melina Marchetta is the idea of searching for identity. Throughout the novel, Josie, the main character, is faced with many issues and struggles surrounding her identity. As the novel progresses, she comes to terms with these issues and learns to accept herself.

At the beginning of the novel Josie resents the fact that she is of an Italian background. She resents her culture. Josie wants to run away from her Italian culture. She hates going to traditional family events such as Tomato Day and strongly resents being called a 'wog'. She says, "One day I'll run. Run to be free and to think for myself. I'll run to be emancipated. If society will let me." By the end of the novel Josie has come to realise that no matter how far she runs to try and escape her culture, it will always be an important part of her identity.

Josie is a scholarship student at Saint Martha's College and at the beginning of the novel she resents this fact. "I come under the scholarship category. I felt disadvantaged from the beginning." She struggles to come to grips with her scholarship status and becomes very upset when people make personal remarks about her because of this status. However, by the end of the novel Josie has come to realise all the great opportunities she has been given by being awarded the scholarship.

Also at the beginning of the novel, Josie has no knowledge of her father and subsequently no relationship with him. Josie resents Michael Andretti because of the fact that he walked out on her pregnant mother, Christina. Josie comments, "We do know that he is alive and is a barrister in Adelaide, but that's about it." But once Josie gets to know her father, and learns about his reasons for leaving, the two develop quite a close relationship. She is even prepared to take his name and become Josie Andretti. This is important because Josie now feels like she has a 'whole' identity – a relationship with her mother and father, and she can now relate to her family ties.

Josie also has serious issues with her Nonna. Nonna wants her to be a "good Italian girl". By this she means she wants Josie to date Italian boys, present herself well to society and attend traditional family events. Josie really resents this because she believes Nonna only makes her do these things so Nonna herself will look good. Nonna feels she "deserves respect" from Josie. As the novel progresses Josie learns the truth about her own mother's illegitimacy, she comes to realise that her Nonna was, and still is, only trying to protect her. The pair develop a close relationship and this helps Josie come to terms with her own illegitimacy.

The title is 'Looking for Alibrandi' and that is exactly what Josie is doing – looking for herself. By the end of the novel Josie has come to accept herself and her true identity, because at last she "understands". (*E*)

Task 10

The novel 'Spider', written by William Taylor, is worth reading as the events, characters and language are interesting and can be related to everyday life. It also raises interesting issues that cause the reader to think and reflect.

One of these issues is the moral question raised by Spider when he finds out his mother, Annabel, is a stripper and used to be a prostitute. Spider questions the morals of the sex industry by asking, "Is there anything wrong with being a stripper or a prostitute?" He also questions the exploitation involved in the sex industry by asking, "Who is the exploiter and who is the exploited?" The fact that Spider is unable to answer these questions is good as it causes the reader to come to their own conclusion.

The structure and language used in the novel is a further reason why it is worth reading. The novel is logically divided into chapters and then parts within the chapters. The parts within chapters generally indicate a time change and this makes the novel easy to follow. The language used is both colloquial and descriptive. The characters use words such as "aye?" and "helluva"; these are relevant to everyday conversation.

The characters are another reason that 'Spider' is worth reading as they are interesting and credible. For example, the character Bryson is a fairly stereotypical kiwi bloke and so the reader can relate to and envisage him. Bryson is funny, down-to-earth, and he is well described. His involvement in the novel brings humour to it when he says things such as, "Are you a real man or a pussy cat?" Bryson is an interesting and funny character with interesting ideas that make the book enjoyable to read.

One of the interesting ideas that Bryson has is that it is essential for Spider, Mark and Luke to be what Bryson defines as 'real men' – this means they are tough, drink beer and go hunting. Bryson also believes that the boys need male role models in their lives and because none of them have fathers Bryson adopts the role, saying, "It's sad that none of youse have got dads or nuthin', I'm going to be your male role model." The importance of these ideas and this event is that not only does it cause humour but again the novel raises issues for the reader to think about and reflect on – this issue is whether 'boys really do need male role models in their lives'.

Another reason why the novel is worth reading is that it has many events that cause the reader to stay interested and keep reading. The event of Spider finding out about Annabel's stripping is an unexpected twist which creates a lot of tension and the reader is eager to see whether the relationship will change or not. The Helene Goldman Piano Competition also holds appealing tension, as the reader wants to know whether Spider wins.

The novel 'Spider' is worth reading as it has interesting characters, events and ideas that keep the reader interested and the reader can also relate to these factors well. (*E*)

Achievement Standard 1.4

Task 1

Answers will vary.

Task 2

Witi Ihimaera deserves his reputation as one of New Zealand's best short story writers. His stories reach out and touch the reader emotionally and this is particularly evident in his short stories, *A Game of Cards* and *Tangi*.

A Game of Cards stirs feelings of sadness and of joy. The story is primarily sad because it focuses on the final hours of a unique woman before she dies. The story begins with a young Maori man returning to his whanau from his new home in the city. It is obvious that he hasn't been to see his family for a long time. On his arrival he is told that his favourite Nanny, Nanny Miro, is seriously unwell. When he calls to visit, Nanny Tama, her husband, cries on his shoulder and he notices small spots of blood on Nanny Miro's pillow where she had been coughing. She too cries on seeing the narrator. The story is told in the first person and as a result the reader feels empathy with the young man, who is faced with his beloved Nanny looking so thin, grey and "all bones".

When Nanny Miro dies later that night, her house is crowded with men, women and children all playing her favourite game, cards. The old ladies sit around Nanny Miro's bed and they cackle and joke as they play. Nanny Miro is caught cheating, and even though her eyes are "streaming with tears" she begins to laugh and as laughter consumes the room she quietly dies. Her sense of character and her fun-loving ways make it seem almost personal when she dies – the reader feels the sadness of the moment, along with her much loved family.

However, the laughter is also a very important aspect of the story. Ihimaera isn't simply telling a sad tale, he is celebrating a unique life and a special person and he wants the reader to feel the laughter as well. Nanny Miro is remembered by the narrator, as playing cards with all the other kuia, surrounded in "clouds of smoke", laughing and cackling and gossiping. He remembers her wiggling her hips when she won to make "her victory sweeter". He also remembers her regular cheating – even when she played patience alone! His warm memories bring joy to the story and leave the reader feeling the warmth of Nanny Miro, as if we knew her personally.

Tangi, as the title suggests, is also centred on death and loss. Again the narrator is a young male who has chosen to live in the city, away from his family. He returns home for his father's tangi. Again the primary feeling is one of sadness, which increases as the narrator slowly approaches the marae. We learn that his father was only fifty-seven and his death is an obvious shock for Tama, the narrator. As Tama gets closer he remembers when his Nanny Puti died, when he was much younger. He was consumed with grief as a child when his Nanny Puti died and he begged his father not to ever die and leave him. He is again consumed with grief as an adult and the last lines of the story see his young self and his adult self merge when he calls to his father, "Daddy, don't leave me in the dark. Hold my hand …" The reader cannot help but feel his grief, his sense of loss and bewilderment.

As we witness Tama approach the marae and then approach his father's open casket, we also feel a sense of pride. He remembers his father telling him, "You must always look after your younger sisters and brothers, Tama. … You are the eldest. That is your duty, your obligation. I was taught that as a child. I teach you that now." The reader feels proud of Tama that he does live up to his obligations. He is afraid, and even tells his sister Marama of his fear. He closes his eyes tightly, but responds to his grand-uncle's challenge with pride, proclaiming his name, whakapapa, and lineage. He tells himself, "Let all who hear you know that you are indeed a Mahana. It is a proud name and your people a proud people." We feel glad for him that he conducted himself with dignity and poise. (**E**)

Task 3

'Daffodils', by William Wordsworth, is a beautiful poem that captures a moment in the poet's life and explains the lasting effect it had on him. The language Wordsworth uses makes the poem very enjoyable. The poem begins with a simile, "I wandered lonely as a cloud that floats on high o'er vales and hills." This is very effective as it establishes the initial mood of the poem. We learn that the poet is alone and is aimless; he is drifting about with no real direction or sense of purpose. He feels removed from the world, as if he is far above everything looking down from a great height.

Wordsworth then comes across a mass of golden daffodils. He uses personification to bring the daffodils to life and describes them as "a crowd" and explains that they are "fluttering and dancing in the breeze". The description of the flowers dancing brings associations of fun, energy and friendship to the scene. The poem explains that the flowers are competing with the waves beside them who are also dancing, but the daffodils, "outdid the sparkling waves in glee". The energy brought to the scene by the personification contrasts the lonely mood of the earlier lines and also brings a sense of joy to the reader.

A third use of language that I enjoyed was Wordsworth's use of metaphor in the final stanza. Prior to the last stanza he uses repetition to reinforce how mesmerising the scene of the daffodils was. He says that he "gazed – and gazed – but little thought what wealth the show to me had brought." The vision of the "never-ending line" of daffodils enchants him and he finds it hard to leave the scene. What he doesn't realise is that he takes the scene with him in his heart. He uses metaphor to describe this when he says, "… they flash upon that inward eye, which is the bliss of solitude; and then my heart with pleasure fills and dances with the daffodils." By referring to the soul as 'that inward eye' he emphasises the importance of seeing with our heart and soul.

Another poem that I very much enjoyed is 'The Road Not Taken', by Robert Frost. This poem also uses language very successfully. Frost uses the extended metaphor of two diverging roads to symbolise the idea of decisions. The poem begins, "Two roads diverged in a yellow wood, and sorry I could not travel both and be one traveller, long I stood …" This use of figurative language is very effective because the reader can relate to the idea of having to choose between two roads and can visualise standing at the point where they separate and being unsure of which way to go. It is also very clever because it captures the idea of life being a journey, a road we travel.

Frost also uses vivid description, which makes the poem enjoyable. He describes the roads first thing in the morning as both being equally covered in "… leaves no step had trodden black." This is a very clear image. The image suggests newness; it is as if no-one had walked either path before. The reader can consequently understand that the decision is unique and new to the traveller even though it is a decision others have made before him/her.

Lastly, Frost's use of repetition is effective also. He says, "Oh, I kept the first for another day! Yet knowing how way leads onto way, I doubted that I should ever come back." The repetition of 'way' highlights the fact that the journey doesn't stop; one road leads on to another, just as one decision leads on to another. He also says, "I shall be telling this with a sigh somewhere ages and ages hence …" The repetition of 'ages' again reinforces the idea that one road leads on to another and it is not until we pause that we can see the impact of the decisions we have made. "Two roads diverged in a wood, and I – I took the one less travelled by, and that has made all the difference." (**E**)

Task 4

'The Fat Boy' by Owen Marshall could be renamed 'Glass houses.' This could be an effective new title because of the image it gives in your mind. The old saying goes that 'people in glass houses shouldn't throw stones.' In a way, the townspeople have their own faults and the glass represents this. They then accuse the fat boy of evil acts without proof and the stones represent this.

The townspeople are hypocrites. They go around accusing the fat boy of crimes such as the fire at McNutty's warehouse and the theft of $17,000 of railway property, without proof. They are hypocrites because while they are busy accusing the fat boy they are committing crimes themselves. For example, Nigel Lammerton is arrested for beating his wife, Artie Compeyson drowns kittens and the vigilante groups eventually murder the fat boy. The symbolism of a glass house also gets the reader to think about some of the issues raised in the story, for example, hypocrisy.

'Glass houses' would also be an appropriate title as the fat boy is transparent/invisible, just as glass is. At the conclusion of the story the reader is not sure whether the fat boy actually existed or not. The reader is led to believe that the fat boy is not a reality, but a creation of the townspeople as a scapegoat for their own evil. "No one seemed to know what happened to the fat boy's body."

'Dear Mr Cairney' by Graeme Lay could be renamed 'A Lesson to be Learned.' This could be a good new title for two main reasons. The first reason is that it effectively links to the setting of the text, the school. The title may also help suggest to the reader something about the text, and when they begin reading, the fact there is more to the title than what they had initially thought may encourage the person to read on.

'A Lesson to be Learned' relates well to what Mr Cairney said to the writer when he was a student in his class. When Mr Cairney was about to strap him he said, "I'm going to teach you not to fool in my class." Mr Cairney felt the way to discipline students, to teach them a lesson, was to use corporal punishment.

The third reason 'A Lesson to be Learned' is a good new title for the text is that Mr Cairney does have a lesson he needs to learn. The man writing the letter, who was abused by him as a boy, has remembered it so vividly throughout his whole life so far. He hasn't forgotten one detail and it's had a significant impact on his life. He wants to do everything in his power to stop this happening again to his son, hence the last sentence of the letter: "… if you as much as touch one hair on his head, Mr Cairney, I will come along to your school and smash every bone in your face." He wants Mr Cairney to learn that what goes around, may come around. (**E**)

Task 5

Wilfred Owen was a World War I war poet. The general purpose of his poetry is to describe and expose the horrors of the trench warfare of the time and to question the patriots who thought that fighting and possibly dying for one's country was an honourable thing to do. The poems I have studied are 'Exposure' and 'The Show', both written by Wilfred Owen.

Wilfred Owen's purpose in the poem 'Exposure' is to describe the way in which the soldiers in the trenches were not only fighting the enemy, but also the weather conditions. The weather brings rain, snow and wind to make their battle more difficult. Owen describes the successive flights of bullets being less deadly than the air that "shudders black with snow". Even if the soldiers survive attack from the enemy, they may not necessarily manage to escape the weather.

Owen's purpose is also to communicate the idea that the process of dying in these conditions is extremely drawn out. There is a monotony and tedium to the soldier's day that is also reflected in the way the men die. The length of the lines in the poem creates a slow, laborious rhythm which highlights this idea.

In the poem 'Exposure', Owen's purpose is to comment on both the physical and emotional exposure the soldiers are enduring. The image of the soldiers presents the reader with men facing the reality of death through the process of war. The poem refers to "summer months", suggesting the soldiers don't want to fight any more, and to keep their morale up they think of happier events in the past. They start to realise that death is inevitable and they resign themselves to this fact. "Shutters and doors, all closed: on us the doors are closed, we turn back to our dying."

The purpose of the poem 'The Show' by Wilfred Owen is to provide a 'birds-eye view' of a battlefield and the grim, desperate situation the soldiers were placed in, where their futures were uncertain. The title 'The Show' is a metaphor. Normally a show is a form of entertainment, but the show in this poem provides an educational lesson about the uncertainty of war and how it reduces a man to no more than a crawling insect, capable of only killing and being killed. "Ramped on the rest and ate them and were eaten."

The poet's use of similes and metaphors helps Owen achieve his purpose as they emphasise the conditions and the emotions experienced by the soldiers: "Grey, cratered like the moon with hollow woe". Owen compares the men in the trenches to insects, especially caterpillars. He sees them moving slowly, trying desperately to get cover, "curve, loop and straighten", but eventually being killed off like the many insects in our world. They are continually being attacked and sought out as prey.

Owen's purpose in the poem is to communicate that many soldiers, including himself, had to come to an acceptance of death. Owen suggests that both killing and being killed is part of the harsh reality of being involved in war. Owen seemed to realise that the world was beyond reform or control and accepted this along with his own death. In 'The Show', Owen achieves the purpose of communicating the idea that war reduces the humanity of man, we are nothing more than creatures. "And Death fell with me, like a deepening moan." (*E*)

Achievement Standard 1.5

Tasks 1 and 2

Answers will vary.

Task 3

In Scene 5, Nana Hannah reveals the truth about her past to Kate, and then dies. This is important for Kate, Grace and Charlie, because Nana has been a major influence to all of them. Nana reveals to Kate 'I made my own truth'. Kate does the same, but Nana's was a positive step from a hopeless life to a new strength, while Kate's inventions are only what Nana calls 'hooey and hokum', or romantic nonsense. Kate does not realise this until the end of the play. Nana has been important to Grace because she has supported her (such as getting her into university, by arguing with the bureaucrat) when her parents did nothing for her. From now on she has to stand up for herself. We see how important she was for Charlie, because he sees his parents are too interested in themselves to help him, so he rebels and turns to crime. The only person her death doesn't affect is Cyrus. He can only give Charlie silly euphemisms like 'Nana's moved on' but he shows no interest or support for any of his family.

(*M* – important scene is not described in any detail; ideas not fully developed.)

Task 4

The film begins with Gilbert and Arnie waiting beside a dusty road. Gilbert is sitting down and appears bored while Arnie is pacing and appears very excited. A large convoy of camper-vans drive along the road, Arnie chases the vehicles while Gilbert watches. A voice-over of Gilbert narrating, introduces the town, Endora.

This scene is a very effective beginning because it introduces the setting of Endora. The dusty road and the excitement shown by Arnie indicate that they must live a very boring and ordinary life in Endora. Endora is a run-down town where 'nothing much ever happens and nothing much ever will'. Gilbert says that "describing Endora is like dancing to no music", meaning it is dull and uneventful. The viewer starts to see the things that may be 'eating away at' Gilbert.

Another reason the beginning is effective is because it shows the way Gilbert is feeling. Many things are 'eating' at Gilbert and one of these things is his life in Endora. We can see Gilbert feels trapped by his obligations to his mother and brother and doesn't find life enjoyable. This is emphasised when Gilbert says to Arnie "We're not going anywhere." This beginning effectively foreshadows the events that will occur later in the film as it clearly shows that Gilbert feels imprisoned in Endora.

The end of the film is similar to the beginning. A year has passed and again Arnie and Gilbert are waiting by the dusty road for the camper-vans. Arnie is sitting and appears calm, while in contrast to the beginning, Gilbert paces and appears nervous and excited. Becky's camper-van arrives and Arnie and Gilbert join her with plans to 'go anywhere they want'.

The ending is an effective one as it mirrors the beginning, but is also different. There is a clear contrast in the way Gilbert is feeling. This shows us that there has been a change in Gilbert's life and reinforces the new-found hope that his relationship with Becky has given him. As a result of his Momma's death, Gilbert no longer feels trapped by Endora and is freed of the burdens he once felt.

Gilbert reuniting with Becky at the end of the film is effective as it is because of her that Gilbert has changed. She let him see there was a bigger world 'out there' and she also helped him come to accept Momma. The film has a satisfactory resolution with Gilbert and Arnie joining Becky and leaving Endora.

The beginning and end of 'What's Eating Gilbert Grape?' are very effective. The beginning foreshadows events and sets the scene, while the ending shows the changes in Gilbert and the resolution of the things that were 'eating' at him. Contrast is used effectively to clearly demonstrate Gilbert's escape from Endora. (**E**)

Task 5

Answers will vary.

Task 6

Kevin is the main figure in this documentary. Carty uses interviews and narration to show us how important Kevin is, in his effect on other people's lives and on the justice system.

In the statements from the police officer, newsreader and judge we learn that Kevin killed his best friends, Joey and Andrew, through drunken driving. He was expected to get a jail sentence, but had to talk to schools instead. The police staff surgeon says that he thought Kevin was getting a 'walk in the park', but changed his mind when he saw how much good Kevin was doing. Kevin is important because although he committed a serious crime he had the courage to own up to it again and again before thousands of other teenagers. We learn from the police officer that this had a serious psychological effect on Kevin, because in the end he was just an ordinary teenager having to relive a terrible crash.

Kevin is important because his actions convinced even Appeal Judges that his sentence was having a far stronger deterrent effect than a jail sentence.

(**M** – important person is not described in any detail; ideas not fully developed.)

Task 7

An important relationship in the film *What's Eating Gilbert Grape* directed by Lasse Hallstroom that influences events is that between Gilbert and Becky. Becky travels with her aunt in a camper-van and when they have to stay in Endora due to engine problems, Becky and Gilbert meet and a close relationship develops. Gilbert and Becky are contrasting characters at the start of the film. Gilbert is tied to Endora because of his commitment to his intellectually-challenged brother, Arnie, whereas Becky is described as 'a worldly kind of girl'. She is constantly on the move, seeing new and interesting places. Gilbert envies Becky's freedom and is drawn to her open, accepting personality.

The event of Gilbert hitting Arnie was influenced by Gilbert and Becky's relationship. Gilbert took responsibility for Arnie's day-to-day care, and this included his evening bath. Gilbert raced home to give Arnie a bath and wanted to hurry back to watch the sunset with Becky; however, Arnie was resistant to having his bath and wanted to play games with Gilbert. Gilbert got impatient and started to lose his temper. As a result he hit Arnie. Gilbert realises how close to breaking point he is with all the responsibilities he has in relation to his family.

Another event influenced by Gilbert and Becky's relationship was when Gilbert came to a greater acceptance of his mother's obesity and her reliance on him. In the beginning of the film Gilbert is shown to be ashamed of his mother's weight and he didn't want Becky to meet her. Gilbert would refer to her as "a whale" and said "I want Momma to take aerobic classes". However, when Becky met Bonnie she accepted her straight away. Bonnie said to Becky "I haven't always been like this" and Becky replied "I haven't always been like this". When Gilbert saw how readily Becky accepted his mother he came to a greater acceptance of her as well.

A further event that was influenced by Gilbert and Becky's relationship was that Gilbert realised there was life outside of Endora. He learnt that there were places to go and experiences to have beyond the burden of caring for his family. It opened up new horizons for Gilbert and Arnie once they join Becky on her journey. Once Bonnie dies, Gilbert and Arnie are free to 'go anywhere' and Gilbert no longer has things 'eating' him. Gilbert must still care for Arnie, but he has Becky's support with this. (**E**)

Task 8

Answers will vary.

Task 9

Baz Lurhmann has translated Shakespeare's Verona to Verona Beach, Los Angeles in the film *Romeo and Juliet* he directs.

While the original Montagues and Capulets were powerful families, we see skyscrapers with their names to show the families run major companies. The young men are still fighting but with handguns named 'sword' so that the lines remain unchanged. They also wear different designer labels – Prada for the Montagues, Dolce & Gabbana for the Capulets.

We also see we are in the modern world as the film begins with a TV announcer describing the situation and showing video clips of fighting. The confrontation between gangs of young men takes place at a petrol station.

For those who know more about Shakespearean plays, there are visual jokes. One shop is called 'Rosencrantzky's' while another is 'A Pound of Flesh'; and the movie theatre is called the 'Globe Theater'.

This conversion to modern Los Angeles has two effects. Firstly, it makes the story of Romeo and Juliet accessible to younger viewers who would not normally watch Shakespeare – they find the setting, and background music familiar (even if it is not their own, they recognise it from Hollywood and American TV). Secondly, Baz Lurhmann shows that the story may be old but is still relevant today – when Juliet asks 'Wherefore art thou Romeo?' (ie 'why do you belong to my family's enemies?'), her question could be asked by any star-crossed lover. (**E**)

Task 10

Answers will vary.

Task 11

An important idea in the film *Billy Elliot*, directed by Stephen Daldry, is that of stereotypes. There are a few different aspects of this main idea of stereotypes – the breaking of stereotypes, acceptance despite stereotypes, and the fact that most stereotypes are not correct in the first place. The film is set in Northern England during the 1980s, at a time when the area was badly affected by the strikes by coal miners. Both Billy's father and brother work in the mines and are on strike. In this area, during this time and in Billy's family, 'boys are boys' and 'girls are girls'. The boys are expected to play physical sports and provide for the family, and girls are expected to stay in the home.

A reason that this idea is so important to the film is that the stereotypes help the viewer to build a strong relationship with the central character of Billy. When Billy becomes interested in ballet instead of his father's preferred boxing, he is breaking the stereotype of the 'common male', portrayed by both his older brother and his father. Instead of playing a physical and violent sport, he is participating in a 'girls' sport', one that is considered 'wimpy'. The viewer can identify with Billy's situation and the fact that he is being stopped from doing something he loves. Billy is seen as ahead of his time, or above the ideas of those surrounding him, he is almost a 'hero' to the viewer. He is also seen as a 'hero' by the girls in the ballet class, and also by the teacher, though she won't let him see it.

Another reason that the idea of stereotypes is important to the film *Billy Elliot* is that it helps to set the scene and the atmosphere of that scene for the film. The stereotype of the working male is very important to the atmosphere of the film because this idea is contradicted by the strikes. The stress that this stereotype puts the strikers under is shown by the behaviour of Billy's father and his friends, and the overall attitude and emotion of the town. The men feel like they are failing their families by not being able to provide for them. Other stereotypes that help to set the scene for the film include that of the typical boy (which makes us realise why Billy's family are opposed to his learning ballet), and that of the low-income family (which makes the Royal Ballet School such a different setting and atmosphere for Billy and his father).

The main reason that the idea of stereotypes is important in *Billy Elliot* is because it is the main theme addressed in the film. The entire film is formed around this central theme, that stereotypes are quite often not true in the first place and that we shouldn't judge people just because of the group they are a part of, but on their own merit. (*E*)

Task 12

Answers will vary.

Task 13

The film 'White Squall' by Ridley Scott displays a number of production techniques. In particular in the scene of the crew playing with the dolphin, Frank picking up a harpoon and shooting the dolphin, followed by the Skipper challenging Frank in front of the crew to finish killing the dolphin, two production techniques that worked well and are important are camera work and music.

The effective camera work in this scene is important as it shows the viewer the characters' expressions and other body language to help the viewer understand what characters may be feeling. In this scene just after Frank shoots the dolphin the Skipper steps up to Frank's face challenging him. The camera shot on the two is a close up. The close up shot is important as it shows the anger of the Skipper and the fear in Frank's face. This created strong tension at this point of the film.

The camera angles were also effectively used, influencing how the viewer saw each character. Just before Frank harpoons the dolphin, the camera looks at him from a low angle making him look intimidating. After he has shot the dolphin and the Skipper is challenging him, the angle on Frank is high making him look scared and threatened. The camera angle helps reinforce the fact that Frank has done something incredibly wrong and that the Skipper is in a strong, dominant position. The camera angles prepare the viewer for Frank being put off the boat because of his actions.

Music also works well and is important because it allows the reader to feel tension, suspense, sympathy and horror. In this scene in particular, the music is well crafted. When the crew is playing with the dolphin the music is cheerful and light in tone and feel. As Frank picks up the harpoon the music speeds up and discordant sounds created by a flute are added to the melody increasing the tension and suspense of this scene. Just as Frank shoots the dolphin there is a loud bang, followed by silence. This creates a space for the audience to absorb exactly what Frank has just done. The music which follows adds to the chaos and horror of the final part of this scene, as the Skipper kills the dolphin.

In conclusion the film makes effective use of the production techniques of camera work and music. The production features are important as they help the viewer become more emotionally involved with events and characters. (*E*)

Achievement Standard 1.6

Task 1

1.	2.	3.	4.	5.	6.	7.	8.	9.	10.	11.	12.	13.	14.	15.
b	i	a	k	f	g	d	h	e	l	c	j	m	o	n

Reading Written Texts

1. a. infectious (**A**)

    b. Promoting Māori development in *all* areas, not just health. (**A**)

    c. Mihi has helped Rikki to improve himself. She has helped him get back to school, stop smoking, eat properly and slowly get fit. Mihi helped Rikki to get his priorities straight and put education and his health ahead of his social life; '… because of her I wanted to change my lifestyle'. (**M**)

    d. This means informing the community about how she is helping others and what people like Rikki have achieved. If they let enough people have this information and gain a good reputation for being successful, the community will spread the word and Mihi will be able to help more people allowing them to regain some control or 'power' over their lives. (**E**)

2. a. Personification / alliteration. (**A**)

    b. A pipi. (**A**)

    c. The other person is thinking that the boy has not caught anything exciting, they do not think he has actually caught a fish. Although the boy is rather anxious to see what he has caught, the other person watching him has little faith that he has a fish on the end of his line. (**E**)

    d. By repeating the onomatopoeic word 'slish' we can hear the sound of the sea move against the jetty the boy is fishing from. It is rhythmic and relaxing to the ear, reinforcing how the boy feels as he fishes. (**E**)

Reading Visual Texts

1. a. Close up. (**A**)

    b. The likely target audience for this film would be younger (ages 20–30s) overseas tourists who do not know what New Zealand has to offer as a holiday destination. This is shown by the wide range of adventure activities included in the film, such as white-water rafting and paragliding. (**M**)

    c. The words and images are linked by showing a number of 'Wild' and 'Adventure' activities available in New Zealand. The word 'wild' is reinforced by the bungee jumping and snowboarding images and the word 'adventure' is supported by the image of a traditional Māori moko on the man's face and the steamboat. (**E**)

2. a. Genetic Engineering. (**A**)

    b. Say no to GE / 'Call' / 'Mail your donation' / 'Exercise your right to buy GE free foods by checking out our website'. (**A**)

    c. The barcode symbolises genetically engineered food and food that is not genetically engineered. The straight lines of the barcode represent the non-GE food which has not been changed in any way. The squiggly, deformed lines of the barcode represent food which has been genetically engineered, or altered in some way. The purpose of the advert is to make us think about and look carefully at the food we buy, hence the barcode. The advert wants us to be more aware of the possibility of genetically engineered food in our stores and encourages us to buy GE free foods. (**E**)

Reading Oral Texts

1. a. Metaphor or alliteration. (**A**)

116 Answers

   b. They are examples of how another person other than the speech maker might pronounce people's names incorrectly.

   It draws attention to the poor pronunciation of student names by some teachers and the fact that the speaker considers this shows a lack of effort on the teacher's part. (**A**)

   c. The main idea is that we should address all cultures in a manner which is appropriate to them. That in a bicultural country it is necessary for us to be culturally aware and sensitive and this includes correct pronunciation of names. You should be proud of your own culture and ask yourself how culturally aware you are. (**E**)

2. **a.** To emphasise how big her thighs are. (**A**)

   b. 'fuller figured'. (**A**)

   c. The main point put forward by the speaker about body image is that we are surrounded by people telling us we need to be skinny or we need to wear a certain fashion to be beautiful. The media constantly bombard us with images of the 'perfect' body but we need to just accept ourselves and others for who they are, not what size they are or what they look like. (**E**)

Achievement Standard 1.7

Tasks 1–3

Answers will vary.

Task 4

1. Use gesture (hold up first one finger and then two) to indicate the number of points you will make.
2. Rising intonation to indicate questioning voice and stress the rhetorical question.
3. Pause before 'They don't' for emphasis. Say the words forcefully.
4. Gesture towards own thighs.

Achievement Standard 1.8

Static Images

Tasks 1–3

Answers may vary.

Dramatic Monologue

Tasks 1 and 2

Answers may vary

Task 3

1. **Technique:** Say loudly, with emphasis.

   Intended effect: To reinforce how 'new' an experience this was.

2. **Technique:** Use fingers to make the inverted commas in the air.

   Intended effect: To suggest that Bea's approach to music tuition was not traditional, did not involve recitals, formal lessons.

3. **Technique:** Slow down delivery, use reflective tone of voice.

   Intended effect: To show that Spider is thinking back on making the decision.

4. **Technique:** Pause.

Intended effect: To emphasise Spider's doubt at that point about his future in music.

5. **Technique:** Say firmly, with a resolute tone of voice.

    Intended effect: To point out that Spider really entered the competition for himself, not for his mother or Bea.

6. **Technique:** Say bluntly, with force.

    Intended effect: To establish that Spider had something to prove to himself.

Task 4
Answers may vary.

Achievement Standard 1.9

Task 1
Answers will vary.

Task 2
Some suggestions follow.
1. What does her 'job' involve? What is her history in politics?
2. How does the system work? What does MMP mean? What do list MPs do? What are they paid?
3. Have we always had a democracy? Who was the first prime minister? Who have the various prime ministers been?
4. What happens to our taxes? What are all the positions you can hold in parliament?

Task 3
Answers will vary.

Task 4:

	Open	Closed
1		✓
2.		✓
3.	✓	
4.		✓
5.	✓	
6.		✓
7.		✓
8.	✓	
9.	✓	

Task 5
Answers will vary.

Task 6:

1.

	Research technology	Source
1.	✓	☐
2.	☐	✓
3.	☐	✓
4.	✓	☐
5.	✓	☐
6.	☐	✓
7.	✓	☐
8.	☐	✓
9.	✓	☐
10.	☐	✓

2. **Examples (other research technologies)** – interview/questionnaire, library catalogue, vertical file, telephone, observation, AustGuide.

   Examples (sources) – specific websites, specific CD-ROMs (eg Encarta CD-ROM and National Geographic), pamphlets, response to a letter, map/atlas, video/film, newspaper.

Task 7
Answers will vary.

Task 8
Some suggested key words include 'Zealand', 'democracy' and 'government'.

Task 9
Answers will vary.

Task 10:
Would not use.

Reason: Chloe Brown is not a qualified specialist in this field, she is a student herself.

Task 11
Conclusion: It is winter.

Judgement: The beach is not that inviting in the winter.

Task 12

Extract 1 – Merit level answer.

Generalisations/conclusions based on the information are highlighted **in bold**.

National is right of centre. For example they advocate tax cuts and user-pays systems. **This means they believe that the individual can, and wants to, look after themselves.** They don't believe in State control and believe the State should stay out of people's lives as much as possible. **Labour is more left wing.** Social spending tends to increase under a Labour government. Their policies are driven by the idea of society working collectively and believe that when people can't look after themselves the government should look after them

Extract 2 – Achieved level answer.

Only information is presented. It is not the *length* of the answer that stops it being awarded 'Merit' or higher, it is the fact that no conclusions and/or judgements are made.

Extract 3 – Excellence level answer.

> Generalisations/conclusions based on the information are highlighted **in bold**.
> Judgements based on the information are in ***italics and highlighted in bold***.

An MP is responsible to a wide range of people. They must represent the views of their electorate within the House of Representatives. They also have electorate offices where members of the public can speak with them directly, for example to seek assistance with a problem that the MP may be able to help with. MPs spend time on community activities such as speaking at public gatherings and visiting local schools. ***Their job is diverse and complex*** as it also involves the collection of in-depth information so that they can debate legislation knowledgeably. ***A lot of their work happens behind the scenes, they do far more than we realise*** and they have to have good people skills and communication skills to perform well.

Keyword list

The following keywords and their definitions are used in the study of NCEA Level 1 English because they have special meanings or are jargon words. Depending on what options you have studied in class or are preparing for the exams, this list is a valuable check on your understanding.

Keywords	**Definitions**
act	Main division of a play. Divided into scenes.
adjective	Word which describes noun.
adverb	Words which tell how or when something is done. Most end in -ly.
alliteration	Repetition of consonant sounds.
ambiguous	Having two meanings.
angle	1. Point of view taken by a journalist. 2. Of camera to subject.
apostrophe (')	Punctuation mark used to show letters have been missed out, or to show ownership.
bibliography	List of books and periodicals on a topic.
boom	Pole holding up a microphone.
brackets ( )	Also called parentheses. Used in sentences to separate, insert, or define meanings.
character	Person (sometimes animal) in a text; their personality.
chronological	In correct order of time.
cliche	Over-used group of words.
close up	Shot in which head and shoulders fill the view.
colloquial	Conversational speech.
colon (:)	Punctuation mark used after headings and within paragraphs to introduce lists, examples and speech.
composition	Arranging an image or page to make it pleasing and interesting to the eye.
conflict	Disagreement, struggle, opposition.
conjunction	Joining word (eg and, because).
consonant	Sound made by stopping the air flow in some way. All sounds except the vowels (a, e, i, o, u, + y in 'my' but not in 'yes').
content	The information or message in any communication or text.
context	The parts of a passage around quoted word(s).
continuity	Movement of action which appears normal.
contraction	Shortening of a word, eg do not – don't.
contrast	Comparing things which are very different or opposite.
costume	Clothing worn by actors.

creative	Writing or speech which uses imaginative and creative language.
criterion/criteria	A standard, or means of judging something.
cue	Signal (often previous line) for actor to move or speak.
Dewey decimal system	Organisation of books in libraries by subject, using numbers.
dialogue	Conversation; script as it is spoken.
direct speech	The actual words someone has said.
documentary	A non-fiction programme in which reporters or interviewers investigate facts.
dolly	(Platform) to move the camera along.
dub in	To add sound later to a film or tape.
edit	Choose the work to be kept; organise and improve it.
editorial	Opinion piece giving the editor's views.
emphasise	Make something stand out.
euphemism	Replacing a harsh expression with a more pleasant one.
exaggeration	Hyperbole.
eye of god	Narration from a viewpoint outside of the action.
fading in/out	Dimming and brightening the picture.
feature article	Deals with a topic from any point of view rather than as news.
fiction	A work which is not claimed to be true.
figures of speech	Statement in which some words are used to compare, exaggerate or emphasise, and so do not mean exactly what they say (are not literal).
first person narrative	Story apparently or really told by a character in the story itself.
flashback	Brief look at a previous event.
focus	Adjustment of lens to make the image clear.
formal	Language which follows traditional rules of grammar, used on public occasions or for publication.
generalisation	An overall conclusion drawn from research findings.
gesture	Hand movement.
glossary	Short list of technical words with definitions.
hyperbole	Exaggeration.
imagery	Descriptive or figurative language which creates a picture.
imperative	An order/command.
index	List of subjects, with page numbers, at the back of a book.
informal	Everyday, conversational language, with greater freedom in its rules than formal language.
irony	1. Statement meaning the opposite of what it says. 2. An event with an unexpected twist.
jargon	Words or meanings used only for a particular sport, hobby, field of study or occupation.
judgement	Interpreting/Forming an opinion on information.
keywords	Words to look up in order to get information about a topic.
layout	How parts of a static image or page of text are organised.
literal	Words which mean only what they say.
location	Place where a film is shot.

make-up	Applied to stage or film actors to make them look like the character they are playing.
metaphor	Saying that one thing is something else, in order to compare them.
montage	An image or sequence made up of many images or shots.
mood	Feeling (sadness, etc).
motion	Formal suggestion offered to a meeting.
narrate, narrator	To tell a story, person who tells a story.
narrative/narration	Text written or spoken in the form of a story.
noun	A word naming any thing, person, place or idea.
onomatopoeia	The word imitates the sound eg: zap, crackle.
pan	Follow a subject by turning, not moving, the camera.
personification	Giving non-human objects human qualities.
plot	What happens in a story and why.
plural	More than one (opposite: singular).
prompt	To remind an actor/speaker what to say.
proofreading	Check writing for accuracy.
properties	Movable objects needed on stage by actors.
pun	Humorous use of word, playing on different meanings.
questionnaire	Written questions given to people for research.
quotation marks	(" " or ' ') are put around the actual words someone used.
reaction shots	Cut-in of person nodding, etc.
repetition	Repeating a word/phrase for emphasis.
rhetorical question	Question asked for effect, not expecting an answer.
rhyme	Having the same final stressed syllables.
rhythm	Regular beat.
role	Part played, real or acted.
sarcasm	Unkindly making fun of someone.
scene	Part of drama or film occurring in one time or place; the stage set up for a play.
scenery	*see* set.
script	Written words to be learnt or read by actors or narrators.
set	Buildings and props used for the set in a production.
shot	Portion of film made without stopping the camera.
simile	Comparison using as or like.
singular	The form of a word used for one of something (opposite: plural).
slang	Popular words or meanings used only in colloquial language.
stage directions	Instructions to actors in script.
stereotype	Representing certain qualities (strong, happy, evil) or types (follower, trickster, hero) rather than realistic characters.
storyboard	Shots planned in cartoon form.
syllable	The sound making one beat in a word.
technique	Anything you do when producing a media/dramatic/spoken presentation.
text	A work of literature, or any published work to be studied; including novel, film, poetry, short story, drama etc.
theme	The main ideas behind a text.

tone	Attitude of a piece of writing (formal, sad, humorous, angry, sarcastic, etc).
topic	What a piece of writing, speech or production is about.
transactional	Factual and logical language in a formal style, written for strangers or for publication.
verb	Word meaning an action or what happens in a sentence; also *be, am, can,* etc; and words such as *has been eating, should have come, are playing.*
viewpoint	Who appears to be telling the story.
vowel	Sound in which air flows freely through the mouth: a, e, i, o, u, and y in 'my' (opposite: consonant).
zoom	(Lens which can) smoothly change the size of the image.